YOU DON'T HAVE TO DIE TO WIN

When you think about me
Don't think about insurance
But,
When you think about insurance
Please think about me

YOU DON'T HAVE TO DIE TO WIN

HOW TO MAKE
LIFE INSURANCE
WORK FOR YOU

Robert (Bob) Shiels

KEY PORTER BOOKS

Library and Archives Canada Cataloguing in Publication
Shiels, Bob, 1929-
    You don't have to die to win : how to make life insurance work for you / Robert Shiels.

ISBN 978-1-55470-180-3

    1. Insurance, Life. 2. Finance, Personal. 3. Investments.
I. Title.

HG9010.S54 2009   368.32   C2008-906782-7

We have made every effort to ensure the information included in this text is accurate, but no publication should be used as a substitute for competent professional advice in implementing financial decisions.

THE CANADA COUNCIL | LE CONSEIL DES ARTS
FOR THE ARTS | DU CANADA
SINCE 1957 | DEPUIS 1957

ONTARIO ARTS COUNCIL
CONSEIL DES ARTS DE L'ONTARIO

The publisher gratefully acknowledges the support of the Canada Council for the Arts and the On-tario Arts Council for its publishing program. We acknowledge the support of the Government of Ontario through the Ontario Media Development Corporation's Ontario Book Initiative.

We acknowledge the financial support of the Government of Canada through the Book Publish-ing Industry Development Program (BPIDP) for our publishing activities.

Key Porter Books Limited
Six Adelaide Street East, Tenth Floor
Toronto, Ontario
Canada M5C 1H6

www.keyporter.com

Text design and electronic formatting: Sonya V. Thursby / Opus House Incorporated

Printed and bound in Canada

09 10 11 12 13 5 4 3 2 1

Contents

Acknowledgements

Over the years, many people have helped and inspired me with their ideas, attitudes, and expertise, while others have encouraged me by showing their faith in me. I wish especially to mention the following, in alphabetical order:

The bankers: Marie Boc, Frank De Donato, Maureen Duncan, Wanda Frost, John Goldsmith, Kathleen Hughson, John Irvine, Ron McGill, Bob Nadon, Patti Neufeld, Debbie Norton, Jackie Reid, John Ritchie, Keith Sharpe, Anita Upshall, Betty Talbot, Linda Walton, and Sandy Waters.

The insurance agents: Debbie and Gino Boggia, Murray Burkholder, John Cercone, Derek Chapman, Gordon Danby, Daryl Diamond, Bruce Etherington, Frank Duff, Sam Ferrato, Rob Findlater, Alec Fischer, Jack Flynn, Mike Hajmasy, Annette Isber, John Kay Jr., Darrell Kemp, Rick and Anne Kemp, Rob Long, Bob McMahon, Don Moir, Dan Monteforte, Trevor Muldoon, Ilija Parojcic, Bob Reid, Ron Southward, George Sigurdson, Mike Storosko, Sandra Valks, and Bob Vaughan, to name a few.

The clients: The Allens, Armstrongs, Bakers, Beattys, Berrys, Bielbys, Bocs, Bonettas, Brays, Bretzloffs, Butteras, Cains, Rene Caron, Chisholms, Clattenbergs, Cocrofts, Craigs, Devenneys, Domanicos, Douglases, Dykstras, Edwards, Fazzaris, Fralicks, Gills, Greens, Hales, Hartunens, Hermitts, Hiltunens, Holmans, Gary Holt, Houghtons, Hutchinsons, Larsens, Le Blancs, Lessays, MacDonalds, MacGregors, MacLeods, Marrs, Masters, Mathiesons, McGarrochs, McKenzies, McNeills, Millers, Milligans, Nicholsons, Nunns, O'Farrells, Palmers, Pattersons, Pentescos, Pinks, Platts, Robertsons, Roscoes, Rotherys, Rothwells, Santin, Scotts, Shepards, Smeeds, Spielmachers, Srigleys, Stewarts, Stocktons, Strattons, Taylors, Thoms, Thomsons, Wadsworths, and Weatherson, among many. To all of them, I give my grateful thanks.

To my assistants: Sarah Buntrock, Donna Cain, Deanna Cameron, Cathy Christmas, Rona Lovie, Brenda Nicolaides, Eloise Schumacher, Michelle Smith, and Sandi Vermeulen, my warmest thanks and appreciation for all their help.

Finally, to my wife Anne, my thanks for her patience and understanding.

Preface

Previous editions of *You Don't Have to Die to Win* were self-published. This edition is the first from Key Porter Books, and will hopefully fulfill one of my dreams. I have become totally biased about the purchase of life insurance, and I would love to think that there will be some people reading my book long after I have passed on. It would be the only immortality I may have.

By the time I officially retired at age fifty-seven with more than twenty-five years in the life insurance business, I was fed up with people telling me that life insurance was no good, and that they could do better with their money. This prompted me to produce the first edition in 1988. It was a book that was very well received. This was followed by the second edition in 1992 to accommodate some changes, including the new first-year cash value "20 Pay Life" contract. Now at age eighty and with fifty years of experience in the life insurance business, I am going to attempt to encapsulate my knowledge.

This final edition includes some of the chapters from the previous editions as they still provide good advice even twenty years later, and will continue to do so. New chapters have been added, as well as some presentations that I have used quite successfully over the years. The most important feature is my latest presentation "Formula for Success," which I now use almost exclusively, as it encompasses everything that I have been trying to accomplish over the past fifty years.

Formula for Success is based on pure logic and common sense. For example, take the case of a twenty-year-old, a thirty year-old, and a forty-year-old:

- They pay the same amount for a car.
- They pay the same amount for a house.
- They get the same interest rate at the bank.
- They get the same return for their investments.

Who gets the best deal purchasing life insurance when age and health are the criteria? Obviously, the twenty-year-old.

What should they purchase first? Life insurance, but not for the usual reasons such as death, disability, or old age. Instead they should buy it with the intention of using it as their future operating account. What do I mean by that? Well, read on.

Foreword

I was having lunch one day at a local restaurant with a very close friend who happens to be a dentist. A couple entered the restaurant and the gentleman smiled over at me as if he knew me. I smiled back, thinking, "Yes, his face does seem familiar."

After lunch the gentleman came over to our table and asked if he knew me. We exchanged names, and when that did not mean anything to either of us, he asked where I worked. When I told him that I had been twenty-five years with London Life, he jumped back, saying, "I don't need any life insurance!"

Frankly, I did not remember asking him to buy any. I did not even remember inviting him over to our table, yet, here it was, a typical example of a person, upon hearing that one is a life insurance agent, reacting as though being faced with a case of plague.

"So," I said to him, "if you don't like me, then you probably will not care for my friend either—he is a dentist."

"Oh, no, he's all right," he said.

Introduction

Many people have absolutely no life insurance at all. Some only have insurance because it is offered through their employer. There are those who have a small policy just for funeral costs, which are getting more expensive each year. There are also those who do have some life insurance. However, very few have adequate coverage, partly because they do not have the necessary funds to purchase the required amounts when they are young and healthy. Unfortunately, by the time they have the ability to purchase the coverage required they often have become uninsurable.

If prospective clients can think of their life insurance program as their operating account instead of the old traditional reasons—death, disability, and old age—and accept the fact that their policies will always seem to be borrowed to the hilt in the early years, they will find that they can purchase adequate amounts of life insurance initially. That coverage will keep increasing in value over the years and will combat inflation in the future.

This book is designed to help the average person with his or her day-to-day financing. There is no magic. There are no fancy secrets. The ideas are all based on simple logic and common sense. Some of the areas I'll cover are:

- simple financing;
- saving and borrowing;
- Registered Retirement Savings Plans (RRSPs) and retirement; and
- some new controversial ideas about the use of permanent life insurance as a "future operating account" and "Formula for Success."

I'll show you how these concepts can work for you during your lifetime. In doing so, I hope to dispel some of the misunderstanding and misconceptions about permanent life insurance, because you don't have to die to win. Many advisers would have you believe that this product is not a good investment. I suggest that their reasoning in incorrect, and that they have not looked at the straight arithmetic of today's permanent life insurance plans. This book will allow you to judge for yourself, and to arrive at your own conclusions.

There are many books and articles on the market that make misleading and derogatory statements about life insurance, and permanent life insurance in particular, but few of them tell you about the advantages.

This is mainly because life insurance has always been considered a negative subject, associated with death, disability, and old age—not at all appealing, especially when you're young.

I'll show you the positive side of life insurance, talk about the living benefits, and demonstrate you how you can use your policies while you are still alive. After all, it is called *life* insurance, not *death* insurance. In other words, you'll learn how you can use your policies during your lifetime, as your future operating account.

Many people are better off than they think they are. Unfortunately, they do not understand simple financing, and do not know how to get the maximum advantage out of their assets and future potential income. They feel that life insurance is hard to understand. I maintain that it is not hard to understand, but rather that people have not taken the time to sit down with their agent and ask questions. They are always afraid that the agent is going to try to sell them more than they need or think they can afford. I'll tell you some of the things you always wanted to know about life insurance but were afraid to ask. I feel that if people understood how life insurance can work for them, they would purchase it in amounts that would be sufficient to provide adequate coverage for their beneficiaries, while at the same time have it work for themselves.

I'll show you that life insurance is not a bad product, as it has been portrayed in the past, and hopefully change some of your thinking. I believe that this is possible if you will put aside all your old ideas about life insurance and keep an open mind.

With an open mind I think that you will find it hard to disagree with most of the ideas, plans, suggestions, and recommendations I make in the following chapters. Do yourself a favour and read the book all the way through. It is a tough subject to make interesting, but I have attempted to make it as readable as possible by using real-life examples.

People have many reasons why they don't buy life insurance (and every agent has heard each and every one on many occasions):
- I have plenty of insurance at work.
- I don't believe in life insurance.
- I don't need life insurance.
- I can't afford life insurance.
- My spouse can go back to work.
- My spouse would not need my life insurance to survive.
- My spouse would probably remarry.

It is not that life insurance is complicated. It is just that people normally do not take the time to try to understand how life insurance can be used to their advantage while they are alive.

In the fifty years that I have been in the life insurance business I have seen many good agents come and go. One of the main reasons for the turnover of agents is that they cannot take the negativity associated with the business. People do not want to be reminded that one day they are going to die, or that they have a family depending upon them for support.

I frequently surprise people by telling them that they do not need life insurance, but I quickly qualify that remark by saying, "Statistically, you do not need it. Most people live long enough to raise their family, pay off their mortgage, etc., and die reasonably well off."

Early in my career I realized that it was not that people did not want to purchase life insurance in order to protect their families, it was just that they did not feel that their already strained budget could be stretched that bit further to include payment of premiums. At a young age there are higher priorities than life insurance: cars, homes, vacations. Many people are prepared to gamble that they will not require life insurance for themselves or their family while they are still young. After all, statistically, they should not die when they are young. The figures shown in the following table reveal why life insurance is not a high priority with the young—and who believes that they are going to be on the wrong side of the statistics?

Chances of Dying within Twenty-five Years

Age	Chance
25	1 in 15
30	1 in 10
35	1 in 7
40	1 in 5
45	1 in 3
50	1 in 2

Note: The figures used are just a rough example.

The examples used in this book are based on data available at the time of printing. However, the general ideas are conceptual in nature, so the relationship between the figures is more important than the figures themselves. All examples are based on London Life figures. Some of these figures are already out of date and therefore should not be used to compare London Life with any other company. You can either accept the concept of these examples or not, but if inflation continues in the future as it has in the past then the message behind many of these examples will become even more apparent.

Any dividends and paid-up additions quoted are not guaranteed. Any changes in these figures will produce corresponding changes in the examples without altering the concept of the relationship between the figures.

If you check actual dividend histories, you will find that most life insurance companies are very conservative with their projections, and usually pay more than they predicted.

All interest rates and inflation rates used in the examples are hypothetical, and used only to convey a concept and illustrate the basic relationship of these figures.

When I refer to young people, I mean not only children, students, and young adults; rather, I use the term as meaning that age is only relative to one's life expectancy. Statistics indicate that by 2020 it will be quite common for people live to one hundred.

While I frequently have used the term "young couple," this expression could easily refer to single people; similarly with other such expressions.

Any percentages I have rounded up to the first decimal point, and I have never gone any further than to the second decimal place.

Where I mention borrowing from the bank, this could also mean credit union, trust company, finance company, or any other lending institution.

Although I use an average male age 25 in most of my examples, this could just as easily be taken as an average female age 25. Many life insurance companies are now adopting a policy where the lifestyle of the applicant (smoking habits, weight, drinking habits, driving record, etc.) is taken into consideration. These examples are applied regardless of the client's gender or age.

BOB'S COMMENTS

You will find that some facts and statements are repeated throughout the book in order to give continuity to different presentations. Please accept my apologies for this repetitiveness.

Although this final edition is mainly directed at the Canadian market, Freedom 55 advisers, and prospective purchasers of life insurance, there is a lot of information that can be used by men or women; single, married, separated, or divorced people; parents or grandparents; business owners, professionals, or tradespeople; and bankers or politicians in some small way or another. The book covers a lot of good common knowledge.

The Beliefs of Bob Shiels

I believe that:

1. People should buy life insurance for the living benefits, which is to say that people should buy permanent life insurance to use while they are alive as their future operating account for the purchase of cars, vacations, etc., and not to think of its use being for the old, traditional reasons, such as death, disability, old age, and so on.

2. Everyone should own an adequate amount of permanent life insurance as there is no better way to provide for the protection of one's family in the case of early death or disability, to provide sufficient retirement income, and to provide a method for year-to-year financing.

3. Permanent life insurance is one of the best things that has happened to me in my lifetime. I know that that sounds rather trite when I am a life insurance agent, and make my living by selling life insurance to others, but I mean that most sincerely. If it were not for my life insurance policies I would not be where I am today. Throughout this book I will give you examples of why I feel so strongly about permanent life insurance, and why I feel that the major lack of acceptance of life insurance is caused by a lack of understanding. Many people are of the opinion that the complexities of life insurance are difficult to comprehend, and that their lack of understanding could result in an agent selling them a product that they do not really need.

4. An investment is an estate value only if you do not, or cannot, use the investment. (I consider this to be one of the most important statements in this book.)

5. It is compound interest (i.e., interest on interest over the years) that makes some other investments appear to be better value than life insurance. I suggest that the average couple, between raising a family and buying a home, do not have that extra money in the early years to take the advantage of compound interest over a long period of time. Now, some people do take advantage of earning compound interest over, say a three- to five-year period, by saving for a major purchase. However, upon making that purchase they have to start building their bank balance once again.

6. Too many of the articles and books written about life insurance, and permanent life insurance in particular, make incorrect and misleading statements.

7. One should keep an open mind and try to forget about all the old myths heard about permanent life insurance. Over the last fifteen years there

have been many developments in life insurance, and most of these developments have been to the client's benefit.

8. Rational thinking can prove to a skeptic that the living benefits of permanent life insurance far outweigh the death benefits.

9. Most people are much better off than they think they are, but relatively few take the time to list their assets and their liabilities, and calculate their net worth.

10. Few people realize the real value of a good life insurance program until they have occasion to use it.

11. If people understood the value of permanent life insurance then no one would ever purchase term insurance.

12. Permanent life insurance is the only safe way of investing.

The next three beliefs complement one of the key statements in the book: Any investment is of value to your estate only if you do not use it or cannot use it.

13. A person's estate is their net worth on the day they die (i.e., their assets minus liabilities). I was taught that the purchase of life insurance is the quickest way to create an estate. Just pay one month or one year's premiums on a life insurance policy and you have created an immediate estate.

14. If you can think of your life insurance policy, or policies, as you future operating account, you will find that the purchase of this policy will have a triple effect. It will provide coverage in the event of a premature death. It can be used as a vehicle that you can use as an operating account, and it provides a long-term savings-and-investment vehicle for future requirements such as education, mortgage, redemption retirement, and other expenses.

15. It is much easier nowadays to reach your goals with the introduction of the new first-year cash value 20-Pay-Life contracts where you can effectively create your own future operating account at prime interest rate as soon as the end of the first year, especially if you follow my Formula for Success on page 20.

BOB'S COMMENTS

When I reread these beliefs now that I am eighty years old with fifty years experience in the life insurance business, it just confirms my conviction of the importance of life insurance. Although I am, slightly, if not totally, biased, I can honestly say without a doubt that life insurance was, and is, the best investment I have ever made.

If new agents were encouraged to purchase $10,000 of premium in their first year in the business, on the premise that $10,000 represents 25 per cent of a $40,000 income, they will never need the commission on their own sale more than they will need it in the first year, not to mention the fact of the bonus available and the conviction or belief in life insurance that they would gain.

ONE
Formula for Success

"If an idea at first doesn't sound ABSURD,
there is no hope for it"
—ALBERT EINSTEIN

My Formula for Success used to be called "Formula for Freedom 55" to tie in with our company slogan. That was until someone asked me how it worked if he was fifty-three already. This made me stop and think. With my "Formula for Freedom 55" you need a fifteen-year window, which means if you are less than forty years of age we can use income. If you are over forty and wish to retire at fifty-five, you have to use assets.

The formula is to purchase a minimum premium of $10,000 per year, regardless of age, or 25 per cent of gross income in the family, which will provide adequate coverage, money to use during the accumulation years, and eventually a supplement for retirement or early retirement.

There are many different investment philosophies. Some people invest in their own business or real estate. Some invest in Canada Savings Bonds, mutual funds, or the stock market. But very few people consider permanent life insurance as an investment vehicle.

What do you feel is a fair interest return on an investment today? Is that figure before or after tax? What do you earn in your savings and operating accounts? Is that figure before or after tax? Would you agree that an investment has an estate value only if you do not or cannot use it? (A person's estate value is his or her net worth on the day of death.)

You'll find you can't earn the higher interest rates and remain in low tax brackets. Investments can create their own "monster": The more you make, the less you get to keep after taxes!

I don't want to compete with investment values. I want to compete with the values in your operating account.

Most advisers agree that life insurance is an important factor in estate planning and their advice is to purchase term insurance and invest the difference. Unfortunately, human nature being what it is, most people who buy term insurance spend the difference.

My point is that you can effectively earn compound interest on your operating account if you use your policies as your future operating account, which is also your main chequing account. I would like to show you that purchasing permanent life insurance has a triple effect. It:

1. provides insurance coverage in the event of a premature death;
2. provides a vehicle that you can use during the accumulation years as an operating account without upsetting the growth; and
3. provides a safe long-term investment to supplement retirement.

Types of Operating Accounts

Credit Cards. You do not earn interest; indeed you can end up paying 16 to 22 per cent or more if your balance exceeds your monthly cash flow (i.e., you borrow and pay back to save for your next purchase).

Savings Account. You earn minimal interest, which is taxable as income, and when you make your next purchase, you lose the compounding factor (i.e., you save and spend, save and spend; if you don't save you can't respend.)

Line of Credit. At prime it is fully secured by:

1. 80 per cent of appraised value of principal residence;
2. 100 per cent cash value of policies;
3. GICs or term deposits.

You pay interest only on the amount being used at any time and every dollar in excess of the interest becomes principal and is in effect earning prime interest after tax in a tax-free savings account for your next purchase. To use an old adage, a dollar saved is a dollar earned.

Our objective is to get your total indebtedness to be interest only at prime, payments on the principal to suit you, as soon as possible, if not immediately.

There are only two places you can accumulate liquid capital at prime without attracting tax:

1. on 80 per cent of the value of your principal residence; and
2. on 90 per cent of the net cash value of your policies (100 per cent at the Bank of Nova Scotia).

All other forms of investment earn an interest income that is *taxable*, dividend income that is *taxable*, capital gains that are *taxable*, and RRSPs that are *taxable* when withdrawn. You pay enough tax on income; you don't want to pay more on your savings and investments. You will find that life insurance can be better than an RRSP at retirement although it is a hard argument to win in the early years.

Points to Consider

Most people think that RRSPs are the best way to save for retirement but never take the time to look at the math of a permanent life insurance policy (especially the new 20 Pay Life policies, where you contribute for only twenty years).

Funds saved in an RRSP are not available during the accumulation years without paying back the tax you saved or more.

Funds saved in a permanent life insurance policy are available to use as your operating account during the accumulative years without affecting the growth of the policy.

There is nothing wrong with putting money into RRSPs if there is money available in your operating account and putting the tax savings back in your operating account, which does not upset your estate value.

RRSPs and other investments are not competition as long as they are in addition to, and not instead of, the insurance premiums that become an ever-increasing operating account at prime, especially if you try to keep your operating account at 25 per cent of gross income as I outline in my formula.

RRSPs: The Truth is Stranger than Fiction

The following is a comparison of two individuals who invested in RRSPs. One invested $5,000 per year from age twenty-five to thirty then stopped, while the other invested the same annual amount from age thirty-one to sixty-five. Both portfolios are based on an average return of 12 per cent, and the result is surprising.

Age	Contribution ($)	Accumulated ($)	Contribution ($)	Accumulated ($)
25	5,000	5,600	0	0
26	5,000	11,872	0	0

Age	Contribution ($)	Accumulated ($)	Contribution ($)	Accumulated ($)
27	5,000	18,847	0	0
28	5,000	26,764	0	0
29	5,000	35,576	0	0
30	5,000	45,445	0	0
31	0	50,898	5,000	5,600
35	0	80,090	5,000	35,576
40	0·	141,145	5,000	98,273
45	0	248,747	5,000	208,766
50	0	438,376	5,000	403,494
55	0	772,569	5,000	746,670
60	0	1,361,530	5,000	1,351,463
65	0	2,339,482	5,000	2,417,316

The earlier you put your money into an RRSP the longer it will compound (Rule of 72). After age forty the compounding doesn't have the same effect.

BOB'S COMMENTS

The first person puts $5,000 a year into an RRSP from age twenty-five to thirty. He or she gets married, buys a house, and decides they can't afford to purchase any more RRSPs; but they decide to leave this $30,000 invested until normal retirement and, assuming they earned 12 per cent for next thirty-five years, the interest amounts to $2,339,442 (trust the math). What if they earned only half—$1,100,000? What if it was only $500,000? That would not be too bad either.

On the other hand, many young men spend their $5,000 with no thoughts about retirement. I do know that most young women have more money saved when they marry than young men do. Young women are normally better savers than young men and life insurance happens to be one of the few places you can save money tax-free. When the young couple marries at age thirty, they decide they should try to set aside $5,000 a year in an RRSP to provide for normal retirement at sixty-five. Check the chart; they would be required to set aside $5,000 every year to accumulate the same amount as the first person (trust the math).

In fact, check the math. The figures seem to be quite shocking but this shows the magic of compound interest. The trouble the first person has is that it is difficult to let the money sit there when there are other more pressing needs when you are young and raising a family etc. In fact, some are tempted to use these funds for a down payment on a house and there is a provision that allows a person to withdraw their RRSP for a down payment, but this money has to be repaid over the next fifteen years, which creates two problems:

1. While the money is out of the plan it is not earning interest, and if it is not repaid it is taxed on your present income.
2. To pay this money back in is virtually the same as paying a fifteen-year amortized mortgage, which means the payment of the funds withdrawn would be higher than a twenty-five year amortized mortgage or an interest-only line of credit.

Money in an RRSP should be used only in an absolute emergency. I might suggest that you may postpone purchasing RRSPs until you reach the top tax bracket because RRSPs are bought on the premise that you will be in a lower tax bracket when you retire than you are when you were working, and that may be true if your income never increased and your other investments during your lifetime are no good. Why would anyone save tax in a 30 per cent tax bracket and pay it back in a 50 per cent bracket? If you had an emergency, a year of no income, or decided to take a year sabbatical and used your RRSP as sole income for that year paying less tax than you saved, the real cost would be the future compounding, which creates a different problem. The tax on the withdrawal could put you in the top tax bracket and the total proceeds are taxed as income in the year of death. Any investment is a value in your estate only if you do not use it or cannot use it.

You can effectively earn compound interest in a life insurance policy and if you withdraw money from your line of credit created by a life insurance policy to use as income, it is a loan against your estate value and it is not earned income, meaning that it is not taxable income.

One-time Deposit of $10,000
Starting at Age Twenty-five–Thirty-five–Forty-five

Age	Year	Deposit ($)	Balance at 10% ($)	Balance at 6% ($)	Balance at 3% ($)
25 – 35 – 45	1	10,000	11,000	10,600	10,300
30 – 40 – 50	6		17,720	14,190	11,940
35 – 45 – 55	11		28,530	18,980	13,840
40 – 50 – 60	16		45,950	25,400	16,090
44 – 54 – 64	20		67,270	32,070	18,060
45 – 55 – 65	21		74,000	33,890	18,600

50 – 60 – 70	26	119,180	45,490	21,570
55 – 65	31	191,940	60,880	25,000
60 – 70	36	309,120	81,470	28,980
61 – 71	37	340,030	86,360	29,850
65	41	497,830	109,020	33,600
69	45	788,880	137,640	37,820
71	47	881,940	154,680	40,120

Would you agree that:
1. There is money and there is value for money?
2. Any investment has value to your estate only if you do not use it, or cannot use it?

Who are going to be the beneficiaries of your estate if you die ten, twenty, or thirty years from now?

Compare Estate Values

The following is an illustration of five years' contributions of $10,000 each.

Points to Consider: $10,000 RRSP or $10,000 premium

1. $10,000 RRSP
   Assume—
   35% tax bracket tax savings $3,500 × 5 = $17,500 and available to use
   40% tax bracket tax savings $4,000 × 5 = $20,000 and available to use
   50% tax bracket tax savings $5,000 × 5 = $25,000 and available to use
   Estate value is $50,000 plus interest less tax

2. $10,000 Premium   Approximate Cash Value
   First-year cash value $ 5,000
   Second-year increase $ 7,500
   Third-year increase $ 9,500
   Fourth-year increase $10,000
   Fifth-year increase $10,000
   Approximately $42,000 available to use
   Estate value is $200,000, $300,000, $400,000 (depending on age) less indebtedness (tax free)

What will the next ten, twenty, and thirty years of inflation do to the value of the dollars you are doing without today?

Actual Figures

$10,000 Premium	Fifth-Year Cash Value	Estate Value
Age 25	$44,396	$595,477
Age 35	$45,574	$440,750
Age 45	$44,609	$320,939
Age 55	$43,161	$236,541

There is nothing wrong with putting money into RRSPs if there is money available in your operating account; and putting the tax savings back into your operating account, which does not negatively impact your estate value.

There is nothing wrong with purchasing critical insurance if there is money available in your operating account.

There is nothing wrong with purchasing disability insurance if there is money available in your operating account.

There is nothing wrong with other investments of your choice if there is money available in your operating account.

Points to Consider

Money accumulated in RRSPs isn't available during the accumulation years without paying back the tax you saved—with certain exceptions.

You get the yearly increase in the policy, regardless of how much you owe to the policy or to the bank using the policy as collateral, which enables you to use your policy as your operating account during the accumulation years, and in effect earn compound interest on your operating account.

This is the point most people miss.

Life insurance is one of these necessary evils. You buy something that you hope you do not need. On the other hand, you can't take a chance that you may not need it in the future, for mortgage redemption, family protection, education, or as liquidation costs of your estate.

Most young couples start out their married life with all of the same dreams and aspirations: purchase a home, raise a family, enjoy some luxuries in life, save enough to be able to retire comfortably and leave a reasonable estate for their family.

Most advisers recommend keeping your life insurance, your operating account, and your retirement savings separate. But you can wrap them all together in one product. With the "triple effect" method you can provide peace of mind along with a safe investment that can be used during your lifetime, with no worry about fluctuating interest or the volatility of the market.

Think of it this way: Would you buy a black-and-white TV now that there are colour TVs? Probably not. Even if colour TVs are more expensive? Probably not. We now have colour TVs to sell, and even though the old black-and-whites are still good like the policy your parents bought for you, I would not sell them anymore. The old black-and-white TVs are like the old whole-life policies where you pay premiums for life and the colour TVs I refer to as the 20-Pay-Life policies where you pay only premiums for twenty years.

With the new 20-Pay-Life presentation and my Formula for Freedom 55, you do not have to worry as much about family protection collateral for your operating account, tax-free savings to supplement retirement income. A $10,000 premium paid for twenty years usually purchases an adequate amount of coverage and creates approximately $300,000 cash value as collateral and any part of the $300,000 that is not required for day-to-day living is tax-free savings for retirement, etc.

Here's another way to think of it; If you purchased a $200,000 house with a twenty-five-year amortization, your mortgage payments would be X amount depending on the interest rate. If you wanted to pay the same house off over fifteen years amortization, your payments would be higher but you would save a lot of interest.

This is what is happening with the new 20 pay life policies. You are in essence paying too much for the insurance in the early years and the cash growth is accumulated in the policy tax-free.

Formula for Freedom 55

Invest a minimum $10,000 yearly premium or 25 per cent of your gross income. If you can find the first-year premium from your present assets or credit, you'll find that it will purchase a fair-sized policy regardless of your age, which will support itself in the second year at interest only at prime to use as an ever-increasing operating line of credit at prime interest (one of our objectives). This will not only provide adequate coverage, but also provide money for you to use during the accumulation years, and eventually supplement early retirement. To determine this figure, see the Appendix on page 176.

Actual Fifth-Year Estate Values

	Age 25	Age 35	Age 45	Age 55
Total Estate	$595,477	$440,750	$320,939	$236,541
Less Maximum Indebtedness	44,396	45,575	44,609	43,161
Net Estate Value	$551,081	$395,175	$276,330	$193,380

By purchasing $10,000 premium from your present assets or credit (for example, twenty-five-year-old):

First-year cash value	$4,859.00
Second-year increase	$8,315.00
Total cash value	$13,184.00

Some banks will advance 100 per cent of the second-year cash value at prime at the end of the first year:

$13,184.00
$10,000.00 to pay second-year premium
$3,184.00 balance available at prime

At the end of the first year, you have created an ever-increasing line of credit at prime for $13,184.00 on which you owe $10,000.00

Other banks will advance 90 per cent of the second-year cash value at prime at the end of the first year:

$11,865.00
$10,000.00 to pay second-year premium
$1,865.00 balance available at prime

At the end of the first year, you have created an ever increasing line of credit at prime for $11,865.00 on which you owe $10,000.

The best place to save money is to repay the line of credit by running your total income through the line of credit as every dollar in excess of the interest becomes principal.

Where else can you earn prime after tax in a tax-free savings and operating account? (To use an old adage, a dollar saved is a dollar earned.)

Note: The second-year cash value will always be enough to pay the second-year premium, even at age eighty.

Total Premium $10,000 × 20 years = $200,000

LIFE INSURANCE ILLUSTRATION
Life Insured(s) Primary Example See page 30.

1. Is it fair to assume that if you were to purchase your future cars, vacations, etc. from the bank that these loans will be paid off one way or another before retirement?
2. Then, is it also fair to assume that if you were to purchase your future cars, vacations, etc, from your policies, that these loans would also be paid off one way or another before retirement?
3. Therefore, all the money would be back in your policies to supplement early retirement.

There Is a Lot of Talk about "Freedom 55": Illustration Using Male Age Twenty-five

Concept: Stop paying premiums and withdraw annual increase (non-taxable income operating loan at bank) each year until age sixty-nine when you will be required to withdraw your RRSP funds. At that time you may consider repaying policy loans.

LIFE INSURANCE ILLUSTRATION
Life Insured(s) Primary Example

Male, Age 25, Non-Smoker
Premium $428,473

Death Benefit

20 Pay Life Participating $10,000.00
Paid-up Additions $428,473
Total Initial Annual Premium $10,000.00

Yr	Age	Annualized Premium Outlay Out of Pocket ($)	Death Benefit Total ($)	Guaranteed Basic ($)	Cash Value Paid-up Additions ($)	Total ($)	Yearly Increase in Total ($)	Paid-up Additions ($)
1	25	10,000	455,851	1,970	2,898	4,869	0	27,378
5	30	10,000	585,477	23,823	20,573	44,396	10,333	167,004
10	35	10,000	772,286	59,814	51,338	111,153	15,288	343,813
15	40	10,000	951,089	107,118	95,868	202,987	20,777	522,616
20	45	10,000	1,185,626	149,537	168,718	330,218	31,341	745,190
21	46		1,225,272	153,607	185,176	351,072	20,854	784,511
22	47		1,264,826	157,806	202,654	373,083	22,011	823,731
23	48	No More	1,305,020	162,134	221,386	396,490	23,407	863,577
24	49	Premium	1,345,861	166,547	241,448	421,321	24,831	904,062
25	50		1,387,347	171,089	262,876	447,650	26,329	945,189
26	51		1,429,582	175,759	285,769	475,591	27,941	987,046

Yr	Age	Annualized Premium Outlay Out of Pocket ($)	Death Benefit Total ($)	Guaranteed Basic ($)	Cash Value Paid-up Additions ($)	Total ($)	Yearly Increase in Total ($)	Paid-up Additions ($)
27	52		1,472,531	180,515	310,213	505,169	29,578	1,029,619
28	53		1,516,254	185,400	336,315	536,549	31,380	1,072,947
29	54		1,560,687	190,413	364,113	569,759	33,210	1,116,982
30	55		1,606,143	195,555	393,776	604,974	35,215	1,162,027
40	65		2,135,908	251,128	816,505	1,087,725	59,423	1,687,344
44	69		2,376,639	274,865	1,056,315	1,353,170	70,496	1,988,502
46	71		2,503,238	286,648	1,192,115	1,501,695	75,509	2,116,234
50	75		2,770,618	309,314	1,493,449	1,827,508	84,996	2,317,401

*These columns include non-guaranteed values. The non-guaranteed values are based on the current dividend scale. Dividends are not guaranteed and will increase or decrease depending on future dividend scales.

Note: The cash-value increase in the first ten years after being paid up is more than the twenty-year premium.

31

Illustration Using 20 Pay Life Policy $428,473

Total premiums to age fifty-five: $10,000 × 20 years

VALUE OF POLICY AGE FIFTY-FIVE

Estate Value   **Cash Value**

$1,606,173 $604,974

Less annual increase age fifty-five: *Withdraw annual increase $35,215 after tax (no tax on loans against estate value)*

VALUE OF POLICY AGE SIXTY-NINE: FOURTEEN YEARS LATER RRSPS MATURE

Estate Value   **Cash Value**

$2,376,639 $1,353,170

  784,449   784,449

$1,592,190 $ 568,721   *Net after Loan Deducted*

Less annual increase

$35,215 × 14 years × 6% average prime = $748,449

compound interest

(Tax free if taken from operating account)

This illustration shows that you could withdraw more than $35,215 each year or still owe some money to the policy at age fifty-five when you retire.

TWO
Illustration of Six of the Sixteen Policies Owned by Anne and Bob

I purchased the first policy with London Life in 1959 when I started at the company: $10,000 life premiums to sixty-five, age thirty, $198.20 per year or 3.3 per cent of my gross income of $6,000.

If I had known about my formula for success, I would have purchased $100,000 life premium to sixty-five, age thirty, $1,544 per year or 25 per cent of my gross income of $6,000.

Points to Consider

1. I was thirty before I purchased my first policy with London Life.
2. $10,000 life premiums to sixty-five $19.80 per $1,000
   $100,000 life premiums to sixty-five   <u>$15.44 per $1,000</u>
   $4.38 per $1,000 cheaper
3. Add a zero onto all the figures on the ledger statement (i.e., $10,000 becomes $100,000).
4. Back in 1959 your manager gave you a tie or a pair of socks if you sold a $1,000 policy. If I had bought $100,000 I might have been given a suit!
5. I was about forty-one before I realized quite inadvertently that there was a formula for success. It took me eight policies to reach my first $100,000 of coverage. My first $100,000 policy I purchased at age forty-one, and I bought my second $100,000 policy at age forty-four. This was followed by a $200,000 policy when I was fifty and a further $500,000 at age fifty-five. Finally, at seventy, I purchased a $10,000 premium, and all of them have contributed to my success.
6. People today pay more income tax on their first year's salary than we used to earn. Yes, incomes are higher hence the reason for keeping to 25 per cent of gross income. Premiums do not have to come from income; they can come from transfer of assets.

MY FIRST POLICY
Policy #3260291-8 taken out on March 17, 1959, at age 30.
$10,000 Life Premiums to Age 65.
Annual Premium: $198.20 (3.2% of my $6,000 income).
Total premiums to Age 65: $198.20 × 35 years = $6,937.

VALUE OF POLICY AT AGE 80

Estate Value	Cash Value	Premium	Next Increase
$62,772	$46,227	Paid Up	$2,267
At age 65			

Imagine if I had been smart enough or if someone had advised me to purchase $100,000 life premiums to 65 instead of $10,000. First of all, the rate per $1,000 would be less:

$100,000 LIFE PREMIUMS TO 65, AGE 30
Annual Premium: $1,533 (25% of my $6,000 income)
Total Premiums to 65: $1,533 × 35 years = $54,040

VALUE OF POLICY AT AGE 80

Estate Value	Cash Value	Premium	Next Increase
$627,720	$462,270	Paid Up	$22,670
At age 65			

BOB'S COMMENTS
I wish that someone had taken the time with me when I started in the business to convince me to purchase $100,000 life premium to 65 instead of $10,000. Then I could have taken advantage of the volume discount (that still exists today). It would have also represented the 25 per cent of my gross income as per my Formula for Success that I believe every young adviser, or anyone for that matter, should consider with the intention of using these policies as their future operating account. Yes, in the early years my policies were always borrowed to the hilt, but they have been repaid over the years to spend again or accumulate tax-free savings.

Compound Interest Illustration

Policy #3260291-5 Bob Total Premium: $198.20 × 35 years = $6,937.00

VALUE OF POLICY 2008
    8% $36,885
                    ←——————— Cash Value $43,330
    9% $46,600
   10% $59,087
                    ←——————— Estate Value $60,651
   11% $75,149
$100,000 Total Premiums: $1,544 × 35 years = $54,040.20

VALUE OF POLICY 2008
    9% $363,024
                    ←——————— Cash Value $439,330
   10% $460,297
   11% $585,418
                    ←——————— Estate Value $606,510
   12% $746,459

My first $100,000 policy, taken out December, 1970, Age 41:

$100,000 Jubilee Whole Life
Annual Premium: $2,501
Total Premiums to Age 80: $2,501 × 39 years = $97,539

VALUE OF POLICY AT AGE 80

Estate Value	Cash Value	Premium	Next Increase
$507,942	$364,164	$2,501	$21,114

VALUE OF POLICY AT AGE 90

Estate Value	Cash Value	Premium	Next Increase
$731,062	$614,458	$2501	$30,220

The compound interest tables I use go up to only 18%
$2,501 × 10 years invested anywhere at 18% compound after tax
(CAT) = $69,415
The cash value increase from age 80 to age 90:
$614,458 (age 90) minus $364,164 (age 80) = $250,294

$250,294 \div \$69,415 = 3.6; 3.6 \times 18\% = 64.8\%$ CAT

My next $100,000 policy, taken out at age 44:

$100,000 Preferred Whole Life
Annual Premium: $2,488
Total Premiums to Age 80: $2,488 × 36 years = $89,568

VALUE OF POLICY AT AGE 80

Estate Value	Cash Value	Premium	Next Increase
$388,084	$280,659	$2,488	$16,163

VALUE OF POLICY AT AGE 90

Estate Value	Cash Value	Premium	Next Increase
$555,711	$470,277	$2,488	$22,452

The compound interest tables I use go up to only 18%.

$2,488 invested anywhere else for the next ten years × 18% CAT = $69,054

The cash value increase from age 80 to age 90:

$470,777 − $280,659 = $189,618

$189,618 ÷ $69,054 = 2.7; 2.7 × 18% = 48.6% CAT

(Compound after tax)

Followed by $200,000, age 50, taken out June 10, 1980:

$200,000 Preferred Whole Life
Annual Premium: $6,732
Total Premiums to Age 80: $6,732 × 30 years = $201,960

VALUE OF POLICY AT AGE 80

Estate Value	Cash Value	Premium	Next Increase
$647,186	$460,069	$6,732	$28,602

VALUE OF POLICY AT AGE 90

Estate Value	Cash Value	Premium	Next Increase
$547,242	$796,740	$6,732	$39,840

The compound interest tables I use go up to only 18%

$6,732 × 10 years invested at 18% = $184,846

The cash value increase from age 80 to age 90 is:
$796,740 − $460,069 = $335,671
$336,671 ÷ $184,846 = 1.8; 1.8 × 18% = 32.4% CAT

As I earned more money I had to purchase more insurance to keep up with my "Formula for Success." (In 1986 I qualified for Top of the Table.) The next policy was taken out June 10, 1985, at age 55:

$500,000 Preferred Whole Life
Annual Premium: $17,570
Total Premiums to Age 80: $17,570 × 25 years = $439,250

VALUE OF POLICY AT AGE 80

Estate Value	Cash Value	Premium	Next Increase
$1,170,014	$775,258	$17,570	$53,267

VALUE OF POLICY AT AGE 90

Estate Value	Cash Value	Premium	Next Increase
$1,688,843	$1,195,245	$17,570	$72,953

The compound interest tables I use go up to only 18%.
$17,570 × 10 years invested at 18% = $487,655
The cash value increase from age 80 to age 90 is:
$1,354,245 – $775,258 = $618,987
$618,987 ÷ $487,655 = 1.27; 1.27 × 18% = 22.68% CAT

Finally, I purchased a further $10,000 premium taken out in June 2000 at age 70. (This policy is the only 20/Pay Life policy I own.)

$117,790 20/Pay Life
Annual Premium: $10,000
Total premiums to age 80: $10,000 × 8 years = $80,000

VALUE OF POLICY AT AGE 80

Estate Value	Cash Value	Premium	Next Increase
$173,939	$91,795	$10,000	$10,768

VALUE OF POLICY AT AGE 90 (WHICH I HOPE TO SEE)

Estate Value	Cash Value	Premium	Next Increase
$263,727	$226,192	$10,000	$10,532

If any one of these policies was the worst investment you made during your lifetime, would that be so bad?

Remember, my life insurance was not bought as an investment; it was bought to save some money tax free, provide coverage in the event of a premature death, or for funds to pay off mortgages or lines of credit, education, business opportunities, etc.; but life insurance ended up being one of the best, if not the best, investment made.

Someone told me that compound interest was the eighth wonder of the world and that tax-free compound interest was the ninth wonder of the world. I know what he means. You can effectively earn compound interest after tax using life insurance policies as your operating account and tax-free compound interest on the growth inside the policy.

Summary of These Six Policies

Total Premiums to Age Eighty:

6th Year Estate Value ($)	Plan	Premium ($)	Total Premium ($)
10,000	L/P to 65	198.20 x 35 years (paid up)	6,937
100,000	Whole Life	2,501 x 39 years	97,539
100,000	Preferred Whole Life	2,488 x 36 years	89,568
200,000	Preferred Whole Life	6,732 x 30 years	201,960
500,000	Preferred Whole Life	17,570 x 25 years	439,250
117,790	20 Pay Life	10,000 x 10 years	1,000,000
1,027,790		39,291	845,251

VALUE OF POLICY AT AGE 80

Estate Value	Cash Value	Premium	Next Increase
$2,949,937	$2,018,172	$39,291	$132,181
Next Increase:	$132,181		
Next Premium:	$ 39,291		
	$ 92,890	Return over Premium	

Do you realize how much you would need to have in RRSPs or RRIFs to produce $92,890 after taxes?

ILLUSTRATION

Our compound interest tables go up to only 18 per cent.

My total premium of $ 39,291 invested at 18 per cent interest after tax for the next 10 years = $1,090,521.

My policies increase $1,556,630 over the next 10 years.

Therefore, my policies are increasing considerably more than 18 per cent compound after tax, which begs the question: How much are you earning in your RRSPs or any other investment?

Note: You receive the same yearly increase regardless of how much you owe to the policy or to the bank using policies at your sole security, which means you can effectively earn compound interest on your operating account if you use life insurance as your operating account.

THREE
More Time on Preparation
Means Less Time on Presentation

There are only a few forms of security that allow you to get loans at prime:

1. 80 per cent of the appraised value of your house;
2. 100 per cent of the cash value of life insurance policies;
3. 100 per cent of cash in bank or term deposits; or
4. Loan fully secured by parents or co-signer.

If you don't have any of the above, I'll show you how to create your own ever-increasing line of credit or operating account at prime.

Let's make a few assumptions:

• You save or spend $1,000 per month.
• If you owe nothing, you save $1,000 per month.
• If you owe $2,000 or $3,000 to a credit card, you pay the $1,000 month to that credit card.
• Your credit card limit is $10,000 and you owe nothing.

Recommendation—that you purchase a $10,000 premium, which will purchase a fair-sized policy, regardless of age, by putting $10,000 on credit card. The reason you would put the premium on your credit card is that premiums are cheaper yearly rather than monthly, and each payment on the credit card in excess of the interest becomes principal and in essence saves you 19.75 per cent after tax. It is better to save by repaying than save by saving. Why would you purchase a $10,000 premium?

The first year cash value is approximately $4,800 (same as saving $400 per month)

The second year increase is approximately $8,200

Total $13,000 line of credit at prime at end of first year

$10,000 to premium to pay second-year premium

$3,000 available credit

At the end of the first year the bank will give you a line of credit at prime. They pay the second-year premium to the insurance company; it does not come out of your pocket. (The policy is assigned to the bank.) In essence, you have an ever-increasing line of credit at prime using the policy as sole security.

Now go back to the credit card you owed $10,000. If you pay off $1,000 you can re-borrow that $1,000. Let's assume that over the next twelve months you have paid off only $7,000 and you still owe $3,000: Take the $3,000 available on the policy line of credit and pay off the credit card balance. Apply the $1,000 per month back on the $13,000 loan at prime.

Every dollar in excess of the prime interest becomes principal or savings, which makes the policy a perfect operating account.

This could be one of the best investments you ever make in your life: increasing coverage, a tax-free savings account, and a method of providing for retirement.

Hypothetical Case

Young newlyweds who earn $40,000 between them want to pay off the $10,000 owing on their credit card for their wedding and honeymoon. Once they've done that then they can start saving for a house. That was the plan until someone like me told them that it can be better to save by repaying assets than to save by saving in the traditional manner.

I suggest using my formula for success and recommend that they purchase a $10,000 life insurance policy, which represents 25 per cent of their $40,000 gross income. I agree there is no way a young couple can afford to pay $10,000 premium from a $40,000 income, but there is no way they can buy a car or a house either without borrowing money.

There is nothing wrong with borrowing money especially if it is to purchase assets. Millionaires borrow money and the banks are in the business of lending money. I must give the banks credit: They are the only lenders that care about your total debt. You can be at your total debt income ratio with a bank but the next day lease a car, apply for credit at various stores, and neither cares about your debt ratio.

However, if you are going to use a bank you have to understand their lending criteria. Let's use a gross income of $40,000:

$40,000 ÷ 12 = $3,333 a month
35 per cent net debt ratio = $14,000 ÷ 12 = $1,166 (paying rent)
40 per cent gross debt ratio = $16,000 ÷ 12 = $1,333 (own a home)

The other 60 to 65 per cent is for living expenses and income tax. The difference between 35 and 40 per cent is your accommodation and if your gross debt ratio is under 40 per cent, the bank considers your total debt to be safe.

At one time a bank would give a person a loan repayable over five years if it fitted into the individual's gross debt ratio.

$40,000 borrowed over 5 years × 8 per cent = $806 a month, and every time you wished to rewrite your loan it meant paperwork.

The banks are now considering unsecured lines of credit at X, Y, or Z over prime with a 2 or 3 per cent repay depending on the bank.

$40,000 × 2 per cent repay = $800 per month
(same as a five-year loan)
$40,000 × 3 per cent repay = $1,200 per month
(same as a three-year loan)

I tell the young couple to request an unsecured line of credit for $40,000 and they are refused. Obviously, if they were going to use it to go to the casino, they would not get it. If they still had a balance on their credit card and have no assets, the banker would probably also decline the loan.

They ask why they were refused when the payment on a $40,000 unsecured line of credit with a 2 per cent repay would be only $800 per month and they had been told that the bank considers that 35 per cent net debt ratio and 40 gross debt ratio is considered safe debt ratio.

They are told by the bank that they were refused because they did not have any assets. I told them they should tell the bank that they were going to purchase the assets with the $40,000 they get from the bank and show the banker what they intend to do with the money and how they intend to repay. This is what I mean: more time on preparation means less time on presentation.

$40,000
   10,000 premium – first-year cash value $4,800
             (same as saving $400 per month)
             – Estate value $200,000, $300,000, $400,000
             depending on age
$30,000
   10,000 RRSP – tax rebate $3,000 ÷ 12 = $250 per month
             (one-time RRSP deposit)

> (which you would not get if you did not borrow the money)

$20,000
  10,000 pay off credit card, saves X/month
$10,000
  10,000 GIC for emergency, future down payment
    $ 0

They now have assets: a GIC, an RRSP, life insurance policy; they have paid off the old bank's credit card, are using the new bank's credit card on which they owe nothing. They are still interested in purchasing a house, and they remember me telling them that it is better to save by repaying assets than the traditional method of saving by saving. I also told them that the more they saved the less interest they would pay, and it is always better to pay more than is required because every dollar in excess of the interest becomes principal or savings toward their down payment or future purchases.

Required repayment on:

2 per cent repay on a $40,000 unsecured line of credit	$800
6 per cent interest on a $40,000 unsecured line of credit	$200
principal	$600

Potential repayment:
    $800
   +366 (difference between 25 and 35 per cent debt ratio)
   +250 (tax rebate – $3,000 / 12 = $250)
  $ 1,416
  × 12
 $16,992 Total
 –1,992 allow for interest on the loan
Approximate principal: $15,000 reducing line of credit to $25,000

At the end of the first year the young couple can write a cheque for $15,000 taking the line of credit back to $40,000, take the $10,000 GIC, and put a $25,000 down payment on a $100,000 house. I think you will agree that they could not purchase a house for more than $100,000 if they were earning only $40,000 per year. But, they are now in their own home and the interest-only annual payment on the $75,000 balance at 6 per cent is $4,500, which is $375 per month—less than rent.

Situation next year, assuming no increase in income:

Policy second year:

first-year cash value	$4,800	
second-year increase	+ 7,200	
(line of credit at prime)	$13,000	
to pay premium	−10,000	
to pay interest	$3,000	

Situation second year:

	Payment	Interest only
Interest on $10,000 × 6% =	$ 600 ÷ 12 = $ 50	$ 50
House: $75,000 × 6% =	$4,500 ÷ 12 = 375	375
Loan back to 2% repay on	$40,000 = 800	200
	$1,225	$625

This is well under 40 per cent debt ratio if you own a house (gross-debt ratio 40 per cent of $40,000 gross = $16,000 ÷ 12 = $1,333 per month). Every dollar in excess of the interest becomes principal. Where else can you earn 6 per cent after tax on a savings and operating account, "savings" and "operating account" being the operative words?

At the end of the first year what have the young couple accomplished? They have:

- a house and are paying less in interest than they were in rent;
- a $200,000 life insurance policy on each other so that either one can pay off the house if either of them died prematurely. Plus they have taken the first step to creating their own ever-increasing future operating account;
- paid off the old bank's credit card and are using the new bank's credit card, with nothing owing on it; and
- put a $10,000 one-time deposit into an RRSP, and even if they never put any more in, but also never need to take it out, their $10,000 will grow to a considerable sum to supplement their retirement.

The house should increase in value over the years due to inflation, and hopefully their incomes will follow suit. The bank will consider them good clients because the couple:

- are using the bank's credit card;
- purchased an RRSP;
- purchased a GIC; and
- own an adequate amount of insurance that creates an immediate estate, covers all their liabilities, acts as their future operating account, and eventually supplements their retirement.

FOUR
Retirement

I was actually fifty-seven when "Freedom 55" was introduced. The government passed legislation stating that an employer had to let you retire at fifty-five if you wished, but it is no good retiring at fifty-five if you can't afford to. There was a time when London Life would not let you retire until you were sixty, even at a reduced pension. When legislation was introduced to change this, I did all my arithmetic and found out that I had quite inadvertently been doing something right during the past years and was able to retire when I wanted.

Retirement means different things to different people and in fact I feel fifty-five is really too young to retire, unless of course you absolutely hate your job. I was fortunate and able to take a special agent's position with London Life and kept on doing what I would have to do for the next three years anyway. Needless to say, although I retired officially at age fifty-seven, I am still working at age eighty. My job has become my hobby. I love what I do and help people with their finances. I love meeting people and visiting with friends whom I have met through the insurance business over the past fifty years.

When people ask when I am *really* going to retire, I tell them when Jack takes over. Jack is my associate Darrell's son. He is only four years old. Does that tell a story?

Emotional Changes in Retirement

Everyone assumes retirement is going to be and should be wonderful. This is what they have worked for all their lives and in some cases it turns out to be disappointing and not at all what they expected. Many people do not know how to handle retirement and they have not made any preparations at all.

It's terrible to think that the government has provided help for seniors in matters like rental-housing assistance, credit counselling, elder-abuse prevention, and so forth. You would like to think there would be no need for these services after a person has lived and worked for so many years. Unfortunately these situations do exist. With proper planning, hopefully, you will not need these services. For more information about federal programs available to seniors, visit the website at www.servicecanada. gc.ca/en/audiences/seniors/index.shtml. Each province offers its own services, so check your provincial government website.

If you want to retire early, you'll need to have a supplementary account to take care of the shortfall in your income. There are two ways you can look at retirement from a financial point of view: You don't have work expenses such as commuting, wardrobe, and take-out lunches. So you could say you need less money for retirement. Or you'll need more money because you're on permanent vacation!

Therefore, you should have a supplementary fund, and there are only two places you can accumulate a supplementary fund without creating additional tax:

1. Your principal residence: You can have a house worth $200,000, $500,000, or $1,000,000. There is no tax on your principal residence.
2. Permanent life insurance: You can accumulate $200,000, $500,000, $1,000,000 inside a life insurance policy tax free, to use for retirement.

All other forms of supplementary funds create an interest income, a dividend income or a capital gain. If you borrow money from your home or your insurance to use an income it is a loan against your estate value; it is not earned income and therefore not taxable.

Some people will agree that it is no good having money in your house: you won't be able to sell it because you need a place to live. Or you could sell the house and rent an apartment using the interest on the money, but you would be paying tax on the interest on capital. Or you could sell the big house, purchase a smaller house, and spend the difference, but again you would be required to pay tax on the interest on your capital even though it may be on a reducing scale if you use the money.

Prior to retirement there is an alternative. Do not sell your house. Set up a maximum line of credit using your house as security and pay interest only on the amount being used at any time. In many cases you will never use the total amount available, plus, when you owe money to your line of credit you have a place to deposit your monthly income from your pension, CPP, OAS, RRSP, or RRIF until it is required for income. Also set up a maximum line of credit on your life insurance policy, whether you need it or not (if you qualify when you are working, they don't take it away when you retire). A loan against your line of credit or the policies to use as income is a loan against your estate value. It is not earned income and therefore not taxable income.

Some people spend so much time earning and accumulating money and assets, but spend little or no time conserving their estate. A person's estate worth is what they have accumulated until they die.

The majority of people are better off than they think they are. Everyone should prepare a statement of net worth every year or two. If your net worth increases each year then you are heading in the right direction.

A common gauge of a person's wealth is their net worth, which is calculated by subtracting liabilities from assets. There are in fact two net worths that should be taken into account: liquid and estate.

Your *liquid net worth* is the amount of money you would have if you sold off everything you owned, including your used toothbrush, and paid off everything you owed.

Your *estate net worth* is the market value of all of your assets, the death benefit of your group and personal insurance, the death benefit of your pension plan, and the total value of your RRSPs, minus your liabilities.

You can't start thinking of Freedom 55 at fifty-five. You have to begin at twenty-five and continue through thirty-five and forty-five. If you graduate at age twenty-five and work to age fifty-five, retire, and live to age eighty-six, which is not uncommon today, you will spend more years in retirement than you did working. If that does not make you think seriously about planning for retirement, I don't know what will.

I am using twenty-five as an average age for graduating or getting established in a career. Some will graduate before then and some after, depending upon selected vocation: You could graduate at twenty-two with a B.A., but it may take you to twenty-seven to get a PhD.

Graduating at twenty-two or twenty-seven can pose different problems. The earlier you leave school, the more years you have to earn money before retirement. The later you graduate, the fewer years you have to earn money before retirement; however, the number of years spent on education are usually compensated by higher earnings during your working years. Either path requires some thought about plans for retirement. I am sure you will agree that very few people give any thought to retirement when they start to work.

It is often a question of goals. Some people have definite goals about how they want to earn their living and when they hope to retire, and they make specific plans to reach these goals. But I would hazard a guess that the majority of people really have no plans about what they want to do when they finish their education let alone about when they finish working.

Over the years I've found that if you wish to accomplish anything you have to do something about it yourself. My formula for success can help you to achieve some of these goals. Whether anyone has ever thought about retirement or not, if you ask them if they would like to retire early, they would normally answer in the affirmative, but that is as far as it goes. I have some specific ideas that may help with planning for an early retirement.

In these days of job redundancy and questionable economic times, does it not make sense to control your own destiny? Of course, all of these ideas are based upon early planning. As ridiculous or unconventional as some of them may sound, I can assure you that if you give some thought to these ideas you'll be surprised at what you can accomplish.

Here are a few options to emphasize my point. You could:
• buy lottery tickets and hope you win;
• hope someone dies and leaves you money;
• rely on the stock market and hope it doesn't go down when you are ready to retire; or
• use my formula for success.

Once you've considered these options, you can become more realistic, consider how you'll spend your time, and learn to:
• play golf—you don't have to be good to enjoy golf but it is easier if you start early and both the husband and wife play;
• learn bridge—it's good for the mind;
• learn new languages—in case you wish to travel; or, most importantly;
• develop a hobby—imagine me picking life insurance as a hobby; I love being able to help others.

Fewer than 1 per cent of people in the world inherit real wealth. There is another smaller percentage of people who inherit wealth, and can do all the things they'd like without having any real regard for retirement. The majority of people have to watch every cent every year to maintain the wealth that they have accumulated if they want to retire early.

Free enterprise is what makes Canada and the United States great; a person works to get ahead. We of my generation are so fortunate. All I can tell you is to plan early and try to practise retirement a little bit each year with vacations, trips, and so on to get you in the mood for retirement.

FIVE
Estate Planning and Probate

First, you have to have an estate before you can plan anything. A person's estate is their net worth on the day they die:

assets − liabilities = net estate worth

One of the first things I was taught when I entered the life insurance business was that the quickest and easiest way to create an estate was to pay a one-month or a one-year premium on a policy so you can then plan to pay current debts, and the remainder goes to your beneficiaries.

If you create an immediate estate by purchasing a new 20 Pay Life first-year cash value policy, which increases each year to combat inflation, you also create an operating account that increases at prime. You will find that a life insurance policy can pay off all of your outstanding debts and enable your family to remain in the same house, go to the same school, provide funds for upkeep and education, and eventually supplement retirement income.

There is no tax on the estate value (death benefit) of a life insurance policy and it bypasses your estate for probate purposes. A word about probate fees: probate fees are not one of the biggest expenses in your estate, but they can be significant (see page 51). The value of your estate, house, RRSPs, RRIFs, and investments are all included for probate purposes.

On the other hand, it's worth keeping in mind that if you still owe something on your house, only the equity goes through probate.

Benefits of Designating a Beneficiary for Non-Registered Funds

Subject to	Stocks, Bonds, Mutual Funds, and Bank GICs	Segregated Funds and Insurance Co. GICs
Probate Fees	Up to 1.5%	Nil
Legal Fees	3–6% average	Nil
Accounting/Trustee Fees	2–5% average	Nil
Privacy	Public Record Where probate sought	Private
Potential for Creditor Protection	No	Yes
Death Benefit Guarantees	No	Yes
Potential Estate Costs	Up to 12.5%	NIL

RRSP Illustration—Making Some Assumptions

Assume $1,000,000 in RRSPs or RRIFs, all taxable when withdrawn.
1. If you earned in interest 10 per cent per year = $100,000 per year.
2. If you did not withdraw $100,000 per year, the million would increase.
3. If you did withdraw $100,000 of interest per year, the million would remain $1,000,000 and be taxed as a lump sum in your estate.
4. The objective is to transfer taxable funds to tax-free funds. Yes, you have to pay tax on withdrawal, but you have to pay tax in your estate as a lump sum.
5. If you are going to withdraw funds from RRSPs or RRIFs only to put in the bank or possibly into other investment income assets that create more taxable income, then the funds may as well stay in the RRSPs or RRIFs.
6. However, if you withdraw funds with the express purpose of reducing your line of credit, you save prime interest rate after tax—6 per cent after tax = 12 per cent before, plus the increase in the policy values—all tax free. (I suggest that no one really knows how much they are actually earning in their RRSPs.)
7. If you are going to leave money, leave it in the form of cash values tax free inside a policy.

Some of the major accounting firms are now advocating the purchase of life insurance on parents to pay the tax on any unused portion of RRSPs or potential capital gains, instead of purchasing RRSPs on the grown children themselves.

Thirty years ago it was unusual to find anyone with $50,000 to $100,000 in an RRSP. Today, it is not unusual to find people with $500,000, $1,000,000 or $2,000,000 in RRSPs, and they are all grumbling about the tax they have to pay.

In the past, financial advisers advocated buying term insurance and investing the difference in an RRSP. The problem with term insurance is that most group insurance plan coverage terminates at sixty-five or when you leave work; ten-year term terminates at age seventy-five; and five-year term terminates at age eighty.

There is Term to 100 (Universal Life) with a side fund that can be invested in the market and qualifies as a permanent policy. However, the premium for Term to 100 can be prohibitive and, because the side fund is invested in the market, the bank will advance only 50 per cent of the side fund to use as your operating account.

Remember that with term insurance the longer you live the larger portion you pay of your own death benefit, as the face amount remains the same. RRSPs and permanent life insurance make a good combination.

Points to Consider in Estate Planning

1. The equity in your house goes through probate.
2. RRSPs or RRIFs go through probate.
3. There is no tax on life insurance policies or the money accumulated inside the policy, and life insurance bypasses the estate provided there is a named beneficiary.

Objectives

1. Owe the maximum on your house. (You can't take your house to heaven with you.) It means less probate.
2. Have nothing in RRSPs or RRIFs in your estate. It means less probate.
3. Have everything back in your policies tax free, with a preferred named beneficiary. It means no probate.

SIX
Good Credit, Bad Credit

This book would not be complete without a chapter on credit. I can't stress enough the importance of credit. A good credit rating is important in everything you do. You need credit to purchase a house, to go into business, in fact to purchase anything.

Good credit is earned by paying your bills, paying them on time, and paying more than is required.

Bad credit can haunt you for years. If there comes a time that you cannot make a payment on time, the first thing you should do is call your banker or creditor explain the situation and ask them what you should do or what they want you to do about it. The worst thing that can happen if you are late making a payment is if the banker or creditor does not know why. They can allow you to pay interest only, authorize a missed payment, rewrite your loan to make the payments easier; you will be surprised what they can do to help if they know the situation and especially if you have had a good record until this situation arose.

They want to know that you know the payments are due and it is not that you don't intend to pay but circumstances (hopefully legitimate) are such that it is impossible for you to make the payment on time. Do not, I repeat, do not let it get to the next payment due before you speak to your banker or creditor, they have to know what is going on. Obviously every one of us would like to think that we would never need to borrow and never owe anybody anything, but that is not realistic these days when you have to borrow for cars, houses, etc.,—even millionaires borrow money.

There is nothing wrong with borrowing money, especially if it is to purchase assets. If you wait until you save enough for an item, you often find the article is more expensive and you have not had the use of the item while you were saving for it.

The first credit most people use is credit cards. They are convenient, but they do charge a lot of interest. The high interest rates don't matter as long as you don't carry a balance on the card, but sometimes it is almost impossible not to carry a balance. It is often possible to clear your balance each month if the amount of your payment is only $1,000 or $2,000, but when it gets up to $5,000 or $10,000 you get tempted to pay the minimum requirement and carry a balance.

When this happens you want to check the lowest rates offered. Sometimes you can approach the banker or creditor and ask to reduce your interest rate. Some cards offer special rates to move your balance to them,

Regardless of whether rates go up or down, prime is always the lowest, which means if you can arrange to get everything you owe to prime interest rates you can't do any better. Make this one of your objectives.

SEVEN
Investments

There are many different investment philosophies. Some people invest in their own business or real estate; some invest in Canada savings bonds, mutual funds, or the stock market; but very few consider permanent life insurance as an investment vehicle.

Investments can create their own "monster": the more you make, the less you get to keep after taxes!

I have been involved in many investments over the years. Some made money and some lost; some were exciting and others I wish I'd never heard about; some were time consuming; some were meetings, meetings, meetings; and I still have a few investments from which I hope to see a return someday.

The way you have to think about investments is that you give your money to someone else and they give you back your share of their return, then the government taxes you on your return.

There are of course capital and business losses that you can claim against current income tax, but you have to remember that a loss is a loss is a loss any way you slice it. That's why when you invest in the stock market you have to expect ups and downs. When the market is down you need to have the confidence that it is going to come back and obviously you hope to buy low and sell high. Sometimes it is hard to know when to buy and when to sell.

Two of my better investments are without a doubt my principal residence and my life insurance, neither of which were bought as investments. My house was bought as a place to live, and my insurance was bought to save money tax free, to use as my operating account, and to leave a reasonable estate. Along with them being the least of my worries, they have just kept increasing and increasing in value over the years.

The main thing to think about when you are investing is to try to invest in something or an idea that you like or believe in. At least you have an interest in whether it succeeds or fails. Sometimes that is the real value of the investment. Many investments are purely speculative and there are two times when a person should not speculate: When you cannot afford it and when you can.

Good luck!

Tax-Free Savings Accounts

For savers, investors, and even consumers the introduction of the new tax-free savings account (TFSA) will allow singles to shelter $5,000 per year in 2009 (indexed for 2010) and couples $10,000 between them.

The new TFSAs could motivate low-income earners to choose TFSAs instead of RRSPs. Why would a low-income earner try to defer tax in a low income bracket and possibly pay the tax in a higher bracket on withdrawal? A person should consider not contributing to an RRSP until they are saving tax in the top tax bracket.

I am surprised at the interest and excitement over the new tax-free savings accounts (TFSAs) introduced as of 2009 as life insurance policies have been tax-free savings accounts for the past one hundred years. TFSAs have some advantages and some disadvantages.

Contributions

TFSAs: Maximum $5,000 per year, or $10,000 for a couple, to be indexed for 2010.

RRSPs: 18 per cent of gross income to an indexed limit of $20,000 in 2008, and $21,000 in 2009

Life Insurance Policies: No limit. Suggestion—minimum $10,000 premium or 25 per cent of gross income as per my Formula for Success.

Withdrawals

TFSAs: Unlimited, no tax, but you forfeit the compounding factor

RRSPs: Taxable in the year of withdrawal, and stops the compounding factor

Life Insurance Policies: These are loans against the estate value, and do not effect the growth in the policy regardless of amount owed to the policy or to the bank using your policy as your operating account.

Estate Value

TFSAs: 100 per cent of the portfolio

RRSPs: Face amount less tax

Life Insurance Policies: Face amount of policy, plus value of paid-up additions, less indebtedness (if any), tax free

Funds saved in a TFSA: While the new TFSAs are billed as a tax-free savings or investment account they could be perceived spending accounts. Each time you withdraw funds there is no tax; you just forfeit the compounding factor. I believe that most young couples don't have the money to leave in a TFSA to take advantage of compound interest with all their other priorities such as raising a family and paying a mortgage.

Saved Funds

RRSP: You get the tax rebate only in the year of contribution. From then on the funds become a taxable value to your estate. Funds are not available without paying back the tax you saved or more with a few exceptions (for example, the first-time home owner's plan, or if you use the funds as your sole income in the event of ill health, job redundancy, or sabbatical.

A word of caution about the first-time home owner's plan: you can withdraw the funds with no tax, but the amount withdrawn must be repaid over a fifteen-year period or it is taxed back in your current income.

The repayment of these funds, amortized over fifteen years, would be much greater than a twenty-five year amortized mortgage or the interest on an interest-only-at-prime line of credit. Besides, the real penalty of taking funds out of an RRSP to purchase your first home is the loss of the compounding factor.

Life Insurance Policies: These are available during the accumulation years directly from the insurance company or from a line of credit at a bank using the policy as sole security for the line of credit, which increases each year. The interest charged on the line of credit is offset by the return over premium created by the compounding factor within the policy. You receive the same yearly increase regardless of how much you owe to the policy or to the bank using the policy as sole security, which makes a policy a perfect operating account. The death benefit pays off liabilities in the event of a premature death and the cash value can supplement retirement income. If you use your line of credit secured by your policies as income in retirement it is not earned income; therefore, it is not taxable income. It is a loan against the death benefit or estate value of the policies, which is tax free.

EIGHT
What Life Insurance Has Meant to Me

Life insurance has been a major part of my life for so long that it is sometimes easy to forget that there was a time when I knew virtually nothing about the subject. I'd like to tell you some of the ways in which life insurance has helped me.

Most of my life insurance was purchased while I was single. I did not buy it for the traditional reasons, such as death, disability, mortgage protection, family protection, and so on. In fact, family protection was probably the last thing on my mind, as I had just separated from my first wife. I bought my life insurance to force me to save money, to shelter some money from tax, and to use it—which is what I do best.

The year 1955 is not one that I look back upon with any degree of fondness. My wife was very homesick for Scotland, and we decided that, even though we could not afford it, we would take a trip back. To the raise the money for me, my wife, and our new baby, we sold many of our possessions, but intended to leave enough for our return fares.

Well, we had a good time, but we managed to spend my wife's return fare. I returned to Canada, leaving my wife and baby behind while I earned enough for their return. Tragedy struck, and our baby died a few weeks after I returned to Canada. Sadly, I was flat broke so there was no way I could afford to return to Scotland. In fact, I could not really afford the long-distance phone calls to try to comfort my grieving wife. I certainly did not have any money to pay for her fare back to Canada. For the first time in my life, I was penniless.

To bring my wife home, I had to borrow $500 from the bank, which required security for the loan. Fortunately for me, my boss, Tom Miller, trusted me, and offered to co-sign for the loan. I can never show enough appreciation for what he did for me at that bleak period in my life. However, Tom also made a suggestion which, as it turned out, has been partly responsible for me being where I am today. He suggested that I should have some life insurance.

Tom's brother-in-law was in the life insurance business at that time and he sold me my first $5,000 policy. Unfortunately, he left the business about six months later, and I never even paid the second year's premium, and I finished up by dropping my policy. This is an example of how easy it can be for anyone to allow a policy to expire, and why we forget why we bought the policy in the first place.

As a matter of interest, I purchased my next policy about two years later. A Metropolitan Life agent sold me a $10,000 family plan policy. That move can be safely included along with a few others as not being one of my brightest. When my wife left me, I had no family, so, why on earth did I need a family plan?

Later, when I came into the insurance business myself and realized what I had bought, I dropped that plan as well. I did learn one good lesson from that experience: If that agent had taken more time with me, and told me more about the living benefits of life insurance, he could probably have sold me even more, and I would almost certainly have kept the policy, even though I had started with London Life. In most cases, you lose out if you cash in a policy in the early years. This is one of the reasons that some people have bad memories of life insurance.

By 1968 I was relatively well established in the business, and I had cash values of $5,500 in my own policies, with premium payments of approximately $2,000 per year. I decided to take some time off to travel around the world. I calculated that if I spent $100 per week, then I could stay away for approximately one whole year.

One of the points that should become very clear in this next episode is the importance of having a good bank manager. By good, I do not mean one who will do what you ask, but rather one who will listen to what you ask then propose a better method.

I arranged with my bank manager for him to pay the $2,000 in premiums as they came due, and this would increase the cash values of the policies from $5,500 to $7,500. He would also give me $5,000 in traveller's cheques for my trip.

Three days before my departure, I was having lunch with my friend Ron McGill. Ron was the branch manager of the Canadian Imperial Bank of Commerce in St. Catharines, and he knew me well enough to ask me how I was financing my trip. He appeared to be somewhat perturbed by my explanation, but professional courtesy prevented him from saying anything.

It was only when I appealed to him as a friend that he told me what he would have recommended under the circumstances. He would have held my policies as security and given me a letter of credit for $5,000.

"Ron, what is a 'letter of credit?'"

He patiently explained that this was a letter from a banker authorizing me to withdraw from another bank money up to a certain amount, in this case $5,000 in U.S. funds. Then, whenever I required cash in Britain, France, Germany, Italy, or wherever, all I had to do was to go to one of the banks listed in a little book, which he would give me, and I could withdraw funds in the local currency. That bank, in turn, would send the draft back to Ron, and he would lend me the money as I required it.

This meant that, instead of having $5,000 in traveller's cheques, and paying interest on that $5,000 from the time that these cheques were issued, I could borrow as I needed funds, and pay interest only from the date of borrowing. I asked Ron to set this up for me, and I went back to my own bank manager.

Needless to say, when I informed my own manager of what I intended to do, he told me that he could do the same thing, but in my opinion, he was too late. He should have given me that advice in the beginning.

I was travelling with an old friend, Lyle Mills, and we decided to leave our banking arrangements in Ron's hands. While we were signing the necessary documents, we mentioned that we intended spending the first ten weeks of our trip travelling around Canada and the United States. Ron told us that, while the letter of credit was fine for obtaining cash in some remote little village in Yugoslavia, where we could have trouble in cashing traveller's cheques, it was probably best to use traveller's cheques in Canada and the U.S.

We reckoned that we should try to economize while we were in North America, and we budgeted $60 per week each (remember that this was in 1968). So, off we set in our VW station wagon with a little tag-along tent trailer, and $600 in traveller's cheques each.

We had a great time: down through Florida, across the southern states, up the west coast to Vancouver, and back across Canada. Perhaps it was the cruise to the Bahamas that did it, but we started running low on funds by the time we were in New Orleans. We went into a bank, and we called Ron. After speaking to both Lyle and myself, in order to make sure that it really was us, and not imposters, Ron instructed the bank manager to lend us what we required, and he arranged to send him a draft for the money. The funds were forwarded against the letter of credit secured by my policies. This is the kind of bank manager you need—one who will get you back to town!

For the second part of our round-the-world trip, we sailed from New York on the SS *United States,* and landed in Southampton, England, where we picked up our brand-new VW West Phalia camper. We had sold the tag-along tent trailer to a friend in Saskatchewan and traded in the VW station wagon for a camper. An interesting insight here is that while we purchased the VW in St. Catharines we saved on the sales tax by picking it up in Southampton. That VW camper was our mode of transportation for the next few months. We spent the first ten weeks in Britain: we travelled from Land's End to John O'Groats, with jaunts to Wales and Ireland. During that time, we were joined by another friend, George Thorburn, from Los Angeles. We drove to Europe, through France, Spain, Gibraltar, Tunisia, Portugal, Belgium, Holland, Germany, Denmark, Sweden, and Norway. The weather started getting colder, so we decided to look for the sun before Christmas. We went through Switzerland and into Italy. There was still no sun when we reached Rome, so we continued on in vain to Naples. We tossed a coin: Malta or North Africa. Malta won, and we spent ten days on that island. After Malta, our little expedition split up. George and Lyle went to Vienna for Christmas then on to Spain, while I returned to Scotland.

From Scotland I continued on my own. An around-the-world air ticket cost me $1,170, and allowed me to travel 39,000 miles, as long as I travelled in a reasonably forward direction. With that ticket, I went to Rome, Athens, Bombay, Bangkok, Hong Kong, Tokyo, Australia, New Zealand, Fiji, Hawaii, Los Angeles, Vancouver, Calgary, and back to Toronto.

I learned a lot from that trip. In addition to the travel experience, I learned a few lessons about banks, credit, and the use of money.

When I went in to see Ron McGill on my return from my trip, I asked him how much I owed him. He slid a piece of paper across the desk: $10,000!

I owed $10,000, and I had only $7,500 in my policies. I had no home, no car, no furniture, no money. I did have $1,600 coming to me from London Life, $900 as my share of our VW camper, and a job to return to. If I took the $7,500 from the policies, the $1,600 from London Life, and the $900 from the camper, I could pay off the $10,000, but then I would have nothing.

I asked Ron if I could make a deal with him. I prepared a budget of $1,000 per month, based on the income I had been making before I left on my trip. I also felt that, while I was away, I had had a lot of time to think about my future, and I knew that I could improve upon my earnings. This was my proposed budget:

Bank loan	$ 200
Life insurance	200
Rent	150
Gas	50
Golf Club	50
Utilities	100
Miscellaneous	50
Food and pocket	<u>200</u>
	$1,000

I asked Ron if I could pay $200 on the bank loan, which would bring down the $10,000, and at the same time pay $200 to my life insurance, which would increase the policies from $7,500 to $10,000. He was quite happy with that, but I had one more problem for him—I had no car.

To cut the story short, I finished up with a brand-new $5,000 car (in 1969 $5,000 bought a lot of car) and a bank loan that was now up to $15,000. The bank, however, was not in too bad shape as far as their collateral went: They had $10,500 in my policies, plus my $5,000 car. I took the $1,600 from London Life, and the $900 from my share of the VW, and bought some new furniture, a television set, and moved into a new apartment. With my trip behind me, and with my new apartment, my new furniture, and my new car, I had a new lease on life, and I started back to work with enthusiasm.

That first year, I earned $21,000. As a result, I was able to pay more toward my loan, and Ron didn't mind if I borrowed again. This was when I began to learn about revolving credit.

I was doing so well that within the next two years I had taken nine more trips. I visited Scotland, Russia, Arizona, the Bahamas, Spain, Vancouver, Washington, Saskatoon and New York—and I owed the bank $13,000.

I still owed the bank that $13,000 when Ron McGill was transferred, and a new bank manager moved in. By this time, my policies were worth $18,000, so before I introduced myself to Keith Sharp, the new manager, I borrowed $13,000 from my policies to pay off the bank.

Keith had never met me, and he knew nothing about me, so the first thing he did was to review my file, and to see my business with the bank.

He looked at the file and said, "Bob, I notice that you paid off $13,000 this morning. Can I ask you why?"

"Well," I said, "I had a super rapport with your predecessor. I gave him money when I had it, and he gave me money when I needed it. But, as you do not know me, I thought that I would start from scratch with you."

Keith, who was to become a good, close friend, and who eventually was responsible for teaching me my "banker's formula," then told me that he was prepared to give me the same conditions as had Ron McGill. I therefore borrowed the $13,000 back from the bank, and put it back in my policies.

Keith then said, "As a matter of fact, why don't I get you a line of credit?"

This was something new. No one had ever really explained a line of credit to me.

"Why don't we start with $25,000," he suggested.

"Wait a minute, Keith," I said. "Are you telling me that, from looking at my assets and my track record, I can have $25,000 without changing my basic repayment?"

"Yes."

Suddenly I felt that I did not owe $13,000, I felt instead that I had another $12,000 to spend. Needless to say, I bought some more personal life insurance.

The next year, my line of credit was increased to $30,000, then to $35,000 and up to $40,000.

Keith asked me, "Bob, do you need any more?"

"No. I'll never borrow $40,000 from you."

There was a good reason for Keith asking that question. To oversimplify, at that time when a banker was preparing his budget for the year, he had to total the lines of credit, to calculate how much he needed to run his loan department, his mortgage department, and so on. These figures were submitted to his head office, and at the end of the year he could receive a black mark if he was seriously over budget, but he could also receive a black mark if he was seriously under budget. If I told him that I needed $40,000 line of credit, but used only $20,000, it could upset his budget, and, in any event, someone else could have been making use of that $20,000.

As it happened, I did require the $40,000, as 1973 was the year in which I bought my condominium in Florida. By the time I had paid the price of $18,200, and paid $4,000 for furnishings, $1,000 for the trip, and $1,000 for legal fees, my loan got up to $42,000. I then asked Keith to increase my line of credit to $50,000, and it remained there until a new manager was appointed to the branch. The new manager saw that by then I was not using my $50,000 line of credit, and he asked me what I thought I would need in order for him to prepare his budget. At that stage I put my line of credit back to $25,000 with the understanding that if I needed more I would talk to him.

The following year I decided to put a $30,000 addition on my house, and I increased my line of credit back to $50,000, and that is where it stood for many years.

An established line of credit at your bank gives you a great deal of freedom. I am sure that many people feel that they have a line of credit at their bank when they receive a letter from the bank informing them that they are a valued customer and to come in and borrow some money. What this is a *recognized* line of credit. Your banker recognizes that you have had a loan that you have paid off in a satisfactory manner; therefore, you can have some more—but when you go to borrow again, you may not receive it. It still depends upon what you are going to do with it, and how you intend to repay your loan. On the hand, with an *established* line of credit, the bank will give you a line of credit that is based on your security and serviceability.

Normally, if you ask a bank for an interest-only demand note (a promissory note payable on demand), they will tell you that they do not give out that type of loan. Believe me, they do—I have one! But you have to earn it.

Like anyone else, a bank has a cash flow problem. It is necessary for the banker to see some action on the principal, in order that more money will be generated, which in turn can be lent to other customers, which helps to broaden the bank's operating base.

Some of my anecdotes will hopefully serve to illustrate other areas where life insurance has served its purpose for me, but let me first tell you a little about my income since coming to Canada. I have always believed in living well, even when things were tough. I have been able to achieve this because I feel that I do manage my money well, which I really had to do during my early years in Canada.

During my first two years in this country, 1953 and 1954, I averaged $3,000 per year. Over the next two years I averaged $4,000 per year, and I slowly kept pushing my annual income up until, in 1968, I reached the heady height of $12,000. That was a particularly satisfying figure. For a long time I had been consistently $1,000 behind the basic earnings of the General Motors employees in St. Catharines. That year I earned $1,000 more than GM's basic. I felt that I was so rich that I took a year off work and travelled around the world! In fact, there I was, age thirty-eight, earning *only* $12,000 per year, and by the time I took that year off, my average earnings were way below that $12,000 figure. The simple fact is that I did not earn big money before I reached the age of forty.

Some people argue that it was easier to live in the 1960s than it is in 2000s because everything was so much cheaper, which, of course, isn't true. While individual items may have been cheaper than they are today, salaries were also lower than they are today. In addition, today it takes a lower percentage of one's earnings to purchase a house, or a car, or to travel—and it is certainly cheaper to purchase life insurance policies today.

When I was earning $10,000 per year I was paying approximately $2,000 per year in life insurance premiums. That 20 per cent represented a sizeable piece of my income at that time. By the time I was earning $20,000, I was paying $5,000 in premiums or 25 per cent, and at $40,000 I was paying $9,700 or 24 per cent. The $20,000 of premiums I was paying in 1985 was in no way proportionate to 20% or 25% of my earnings. In fact, I had a problem: in order to follow my formula I had to buy more insurance or else earn less money. So I bought more insurance.

Some financial advisers recommend that you should set aside 10 per cent of your gross income for savings (George S. Clason's *The Richest Man in Babylon* is a good example). This can be very difficult when you have a young family, a big mortgage, and you're not earning as much as you'd like. Nevertheless, I think that most people will agree that the idea is sound. My method, however, has been to try to set aside between 20 and 25 per cent of my gross income, and to use that as my savings and operating account. With all the needs and priorities for money during your lifetime, it is hard to save any money at all, especially in the early years. In most cases, a savings account is not a true savings account—it is a temporary savings account. You save only until you spend, and each time you spend you lose the interest—not to mention the compound interest, which makes a policy a perfect operating account. If you have any savings in the policy it does not attract tax, and if you have to use your savings temporarily you do not upset the normal increase in the policy because, if and when you replace the money, it is just as if you had never borrowed at all. Therein lies the real value of a policy that allows you the luxury of borrowing from your own tax-free savings account and replacing it on your own repayment terms, if and when possible. In other words, you save for future purchases by replacing the old capital in your savings and operating account.

The 20 to 25 per cent figure has always been sufficient to provide me with the necessary collateral or cash to cover my requirements, not to mention that it has provided me with ample protection. In your early years of earning, it would be difficult to consider 25 per cent of your income paying for premiums without the assistance of the bank.

Here are some figures to consider if you intend to use your policies as your future operating account:

Gross Income ($)	10%	20%	25%
30,000	$ 3,000	$ 6,000	$ 7,500
40,000	4,000	8,000	10,000
50,000	5,000	10,000	12,500
100,000	10,000	20,000	25,000

In 1986 London Life introduced the First-year Cash Value 20 Payment Life Policy, and I am sure that other companies have a similar product. Instead of taking ten years to break even to the annual premium paid, you now break even in the third year, which is perfect to use in conjunction with using your life insurance policies as your operating account. With premiums of $2,000 you would have approximately 20,000 in your policies within ten years; $3,000 in premiums more than $30,000; $5,000 more than $50,000, and of course $10,000 means more than $100,000. With the exception of your mortgage, you would likely never owe more than that figure at any one time. Therefore, the sooner you can get the cash value of your policies to the point where they will cover your future borrowing requirements, the sooner you can become your own banker. I have found that it usually takes a transition period of four to five years to reach the point where you deal only with your policies.

As you can see, it does not take very long before there are sufficient funds in your policies to pay off your bank loan and you become your own banker by using the funds available in your policies as a line of credit.

One of my favourite stories is of the time I arranged to have a Christmas party in July. It was in 1972, and at that time I was paying $5,000 in annual premiums and my policies increased by $5,500 that year. I borrowed $5,000 from the policies, and with money I brought the members of my immediate family over to Canada for a holiday. There were nine visitors in all: my brother, his wife, and their three children; and my sister, her husband, and their two children. They all came on a charter flight, with the children flying at half-price so the total cost was reduced.

I rented a house in St. Catharines from friends who were on vacation, and hired a housekeeper to cook and clean so my family could fully enjoy their vacation. We did all the tourist things including Niagara Falls, but the highlight of the trip was the Christmas party in July. Sounds odd, right? Well, I was never in Scotland for the holidays and my family was never here, so why not have the party in July, when everyone was together?

We started off with a traditional sit-down Christmas dinner: turkey, plum pudding, and all the trimmings. Then my friends came to join in the celebration, for a gathering of about forty people. We had a Christmas tree, decorations, Santa Claus, and presents for everyone. It was quite a memorable event. We were even written up in the local paper.

The point of my story is that when people came to me and said, "Bob, that was very generous of you, to spend all that money on your family." I was able to say, "Well, actually, it was their money that I was spending."

Who were the beneficiaries on my life insurance at that time when I was single? My brother and my sister.

As I have been telling you all along: You don't have to die to win—I attended the party!

By 1972, I had been married for eight years, separated for six years, and divorced for six years. I had no thought of remarrying. In fact, I had made a point of dating several different women because I didn't want to get serious. However; with my family coming over for three weeks, I didn't feel that I could turn up with a different woman each day. I therefore asked one of my girlfriends, Anne, to be my date for the three weeks. These three weeks changed my plans for remaining single. Anne was just great, and I don't know what I would have done without her. Five months later we were engaged. Six months later we had bought a house. Seven months later we were married!

Consequently, Anne became the beneficiary of my life insurance. As I have already told you, I believe in living well. I also believe in my wife living well. During the first year of our marriage I bought Anne a mink stole. The following year I bought her a full-length mink coat. A year after that I got away with a mink hat.

"Good old generous Bob."

No, not really. In fact it was Anne's money that I was spending. If I die owing the bank or my policies for the things that Anne and I were enjoying, then the amount owing would be taken from her proceeds.

Similarly, why do you think I drove loaded Cadillacs? The answer is simple: If Anne is going to end up with enough money to be able to come to my funeral in such a car, why should we not have the car before I die, while we can both enjoy it? So, if I die tomorrow, as my beneficiary she will receive my life insurance *less* the cost of the Cadillac, but in the meantime we can both drive the car.

There have been other events that my life insurance policies have allowed me to enjoy. A good example was my fiftieth birthday, which to me was a momentous occasion to be celebrated in style. I settled on a garden party at my home, and put a marquee up in our yard in case of rain. The party started at 2:00 p.m. and went on until the wee hours. In honour of my Scottish heritage I decided upon traditional food, and had a fish and chip wagon parked behind my home serve fish and chips as well as deep-fried meat pies. One of my friends remarked, "This is Bob's version of surf-and-turf: haddock and meat pies!" In any event, it was well received by the two hundred guests. For me, one of the highlights of that day was when the fourteen-year-old son of one of my clients played "Happy Birthday" on the bagpipes—not the easiest thing to do.

It is memories and gatherings like these that make life worthwhile for me; sharing good times with good friends.

In 1970 I flew to Scotland for the weekend just on a whim. There was no particular reason for going. I just felt like it. How did I manage it? Well, let me backtrack, and explain a little more about my own policies.

While I now pay $36,000 per year in premiums, it took me from the age of thirty until I was thirty-eight, and a total of seven policies, to reach my first $100,000 of life insurance coverage (including paid-up additions). The order of purchase was $10,000, $10,000, $25,000, $5,000, $10,000, and finally $30,000, for total premiums approximately $2,000 per year. It is that first $10,000 that I am going to discuss here.

I bought that $10,000 when I first started with London Life. My feeling was that if I was going to sell life insurance then I should have some myself. The premium was $198.20 per year, and in these early years that policy was purely protection. It was used as collateral. It was borrowed from, and put back in. In 1968–69 I used it all to help pay off what I owed for my world trip; however, one of the nice things about insurance policies is that you can borrow from them when in need, and you can also put the money back at a later date, just as if you had not touched it. The normal annual increase is not affected if the money is borrowed temporarily.

That first $10,000 policy has enabled me to do more over these few years than many people do in a lifetime, and if this does not illustrate the living benefits of life insurance, then I do not know what will.

By 1970 my first $10,000 policy, purchased in 1959, was worth $10,000 plus $589 in dividends, for a total of $10,589 death benefit, and had a cash value of $2,159. (Keep these two figures in mind.) I borrowed

$500 from the policy, paid $180 for a charter flight to Scotland, and had $320 left to spend during my jet-setting weekend.

That started a rather important trend for me, one that I have followed with almost monotonous regularity to this day. Let me explain. The annual premium for that $10,000 is $198.20. For the sake of simplicity, let us round that off to $200. Ever since 1970 I paid my $200 per year, and every second year I borrowed back $500—and I purposely did not repay that $500. Where else can you deposit $200 one year, deposit another $200 the next year, then withdraw $500 (and remember that I am not even mentioning the insurance value)?

Often, when I tell people about the ability to borrow money from their policies, I am told, "Yes, but you have to pay it back."

I ask them if they are asking me, or telling me, and frequently their response is, "Well, you do. Don't you?"

"No. You don't!" If you don't it is deducted from your estate and you have the opportunity of repaying it at a later date if you wish.

Of course, it would pay me to repay that loan, as I would not be charged the compound interest on the loan. On this policy though, I purposely did not pay anything, and I use it as an example of how a policy can increase sufficiently every two years to pay me an extra $100, and at the same time support the compounding interest on the compounding loan.

Two years later, I borrowed from that policy again. This time I needed $700 (although $500 had been a convenient sum, it is normally possible to borrow more should a special occasion arise). This was certainly a special occasion: The first Canada–Russia hockey series in Moscow. Do you remember it? Will you ever forget it? Well, I was there, and I am not even a real hockey fan. It is a long and, I think, interesting story, and should I ever get down to writing my memoirs, then that trip, and all that led up to it, will be one of the highlights. However, for the purpose of this book, suffice it to say that the only way in which I could even think about making that trip was because I had the policy from which I could borrow the money. I say "borrow," but in fact I should have said "take."

In 1974 I used the money to buy a dishwasher, and in 1976 while on holiday in Scotland my wife and I were able to purchase matching kilts. The money I took in 1978 purchased an executive package for the Canadian Open at Glen Abbey. In 1980, I bought Anne a piano from a friend who was moving from her house into an apartment. At least Anne could play the piano, which is more than can be said for me and my next purchase in 1982, when I bought a set of bagpipes. At this time, I cannot even blow them, let alone get a tune out of them. But, one of these days...

By 1984 I decided to take a new tack. Fourteen years earlier, I had purchased a $100,000 policy at a premium cost of $2,501 per year. Through that policy, I now pay $5,000 in premiums every two years, and take out $6,000. With the first $6,000 that I withdrew in 1984, I repaid the money and the compound interest that I had been borrowing from my $10,000 policy since 1970, which amounted to $3,700 (six times $500, and one year when I borrowed $700) and $1,900 interest. So, in one fell swoop, I cleared up all the borrowing on that old 1959 policy, and we have started afresh on our two-year spending extravagance, but this time with $6,000 instead of $500.

The important point is that none of that borrowed money had to be paid back, but if your circumstances are such that you can afford to do so, then why not pay it back until you need it again? Hopefully, this will illustrate that you do not have to do without in order to own life insurance, but that with life insurance you can afford to owe money without it affecting your priorities.

You may be wondering just what was happening to that 1959 $10,000 policy while I was borrowing that money between 1970 and 1982. Well, in 1983 before I paid back any of the borrowed money, I got a statement detailing the policy's status as of March of that year (see statement on page 72). What this shows is that by that date, the death benefit would have been the original $10,000 plus $11,013 paid-up additions, for a total of $21,013; however, as I had been borrowing from the policy over the years, my indebtedness including interest was $5,641. Therefore, in the event of my death, the company would have paid out $21,013 less $5,641 for a total of $15,372. But remember, in 1970 the total death benefit was only $10,589, whereas in 1983 it was $15,372—and I had had the use of that $3,700 over the years.

Another figure on that statement is called the net cash value: the amount of money that you receive if you decide that you no longer want to keep the policy and surrender it. In this case, the amount was $2,801. In 1970 that net cash value had been $2,159, and since then I had been withdrawing $250 per year for every $200 I had been depositing. Who can tell me that permanent life insurance isn't good?

There are other interesting figures on that statement. For example, the dividend declared in March 1983 was $280.90, while the premium was still the original $198.20. The cash value increased by $220, and the increase in cash value of paid-up additions was approximately $310, and these figures, along with the dividend, come to a total of approximately $810. How many of you would not be prepared to pay $198.20 this year in return for $810, not to mention the benefit of the insurance?

With the benefit of hindsight, it is now so easy to see what I should have done back in 1959: I should have sold myself a $100,000 policy. It would have cost me $1,544, or $15.44 per $1,000, which would have been $4.38 per $1,000 cheaper than I paid for the $10,000 policy. By using the same system as for the $10,000 policy, in 1983 the figures for the $100,000 policy would have looked something like this:

Death benefit or estate value	$100,000
Paid-up additions	110,131
Total benefit	$210,131
Loan of $37,000, plus interest	(56,410)
Paid to estate in event of death	$153,721

Alive, I would have a net cash value of $28,010 in tax-free savings, and would be able to shelter a further $56,410 without tax.

MAR 02 83 7-688-119 COVERAGE

POL DATE MAR 17 59   AGE 30 ADMITTED   326029-5

MR ROBERT SHIELS

BORN   JUN 11 29   AMT PREM CEASES

COV EXP

L PREM TO 65 ANN DIV 10,000.00   198.20 1994

2009

PD UP ADDNS   11,013.18

     7-688-119 PREMIUM 326029-5   MR   ROBERT SHIELS

DPTMAR 17 84

     7-668-119 DIVIDEND 326029-5   MR   ROBERT SHIELS

*INCLUDES ANNIV AT MAR 17 83

PD UP ADDNS   11,013.81   ANN DIV PU ADD

                 DECLARED MAR 17 83   280.90

     MAR 02 83   70688-119 CASH VALUE   326029-5

MR ROBERT SHIELS

BASIC CASH VALUE   4,170.00

ADDNL BENEFITS 3,874.77   BASIC CV INCREASE 220.00

                 APPROX. INCREASE IN CASH VALUE

PREM REFUNDED 222.70 OF PAID UP ADDITIONS:

```
309.98
INDEBTEDNESS    5,641.215
NET CASH VALUE MAR 17 83    2,801.76;
     7-688-119 LOAN    3260291-5    MR        ROBERT
SHIELS
CASH LOAN    5,641.21
INT AT 6.00%              .00
CASH LOAN BAL  5,641.21
```

With $210,131 coverage, and owing $56,410 on that policy, I would not have needed to go out at age fifty and purchase another $200,000 of permanent life insurance with a premium of $6,700. It hurts have to pay income tax on interest income when you could save money by repaying old policy loans.

There are many parents and grandparents who are paying income tax on interest income, but it seems that even more and more young people are also being hit with that tax. This is probably due to the progressive income tax system in Canada. Today, many young people pay more income tax on their first-year income than people used to earn twenty to twenty-five years ago, therefore; it is essential that one makes use of any legitimate methods to reduce one's taxes.

Few people think of permanent life insurance as a tax-free savings account. On the surface it may appear to be unfair to allow savings to accumulate basically tax free inside a life insurance policy, but there is a reason for this. Life insurance receives special treatment in order to encourage people to provide for their dependants in the event of premature death, and also to assist them to supplement their retirement income. Should life insurance ever become unattractive, then people would purchase less, and the result would be that the government would have more destitute spouses, children, and elderly people to look after. This is why the death benefit of a life insurance policy is not taxable. However, should you ever cash in a policy, and the money you receive exceeds the money that you have paid in (your cost base), then that difference is classed as a taxable gain. I like this piece of legislation: It allows you to borrow from your policy and die still owing that loan. It means that you can have the use of your money while you are alive, and at the same time have your dependants protected should you die. Tax levied on the interest generated from, say, a $250,000 life insurance policy in the following year would probably not be too great a hardship for your dependants.

If you intend to use your policies as your future savings and operating account then I strongly recommend that your premiums should be 20 to 25 per cent of your gross income. Consider what that principle has done for me!

Over the years I have been accused of thinking and feeling and stating that life insurance is not just the best investment, it is the *only* investment for the average person. Many people have told me that I do not benefit from capital gains. This is true, and I have thought about it often, but I could never quite find that particular something where I might make a capital gain—until some two-bedroom condominiums came on the market in 1980 in St. Catharines for $17,500 each. This was it. My opportunity. A bankruptcy sale. I would buy two for an investment of $35,000, and as soon as they were all sold the price would increase and I would make my capital gain.

I mentioned my great idea to my wife Anne and was surprised when she hit me with all my own philosophies that I had been using on others for years. If you have read this far you will know that one of my philosophies is that an investment is an estate value only if you do not, or cannot, use it. When you analyze that statement you will find that it makes a great deal of sense.

So, I told Anne that I was thinking seriously about buying two of the condominiums.

"Bob," she said, "if you invest $35,000 in these condos, and you die, what will the estate value be?"

"$35,000."

"Oh! Your $35,000?"

"Well, yes. But I am not going to die."

"Fine," said Anne. "Let's keep you alive, and we will move along five years from now and assume that the condos are now worth $80,000. You could make a capital gain of $45,000, but half of the capital gain would be taxable, therefore; you would have to pay tax on $22,500. What would your estate value be?" (The rules for capital gains have changed since the time of writing, and who knows when they will change again, but there *will* be some tax to pay.)

"$80,000 less tax, for a total of something less than $80,000."

"Now," said Anne, "did you ever live in these condos?"

"No."

Well, of course, Anne was correct. An investment is a value to your estate only if you do not, or cannot, use it. So, let me tell you just what I did with my $35,000. I used it to purchase another $200,000 of permanent life insurance at age fifty, with a premium of $6,700 per year.

Let us take a look at the estate value at the time of purchase:

$35,000 − $6,700 = $28,300
$28,300 + $200,000 life insurance = $228,300

Which one was the best estate value?
The following year the $28,300 earned interest to help to pay the second-year premium.

$28,300 + 11% = $31,130
$31,130 − $6,700 second-year premium = $25,430

The estate value?

$25,430 + $200,000 + $2,660 additions = $228,090

There is sufficient money in this fund to pay the $200,000 policy to the eighth year, at which stage the cash value and the estate value both increase each year, with no further premiums required.

If I am going to invest in something that I cannot use, then I am better off buying life insurance, after all, it could be a long time before the condos would be worth $200,000—if ever.

If you take care of dying by having a substantial life insurance program, and take care of retirement with maximum RRSPs plus the cash available in your policies, then the only other investments you need are investments in your lifestyle—bigger cars, better holidays, the best golf clubs, and two squash racquets (in case you break one during a game!)—and is that not what it is all about?

BOB'S COMMENTS

When I think about all the things we have been able to accomplish over the years with the use of our life insurance policies it brings back a lot of wonderful memories. I often say that "I could die tomorrow not feeling cheated." I have done most of the things in my life that I have wanted to do. Anne does not like to hear me saying; however, I am still here and hope to enjoy many more years. In fact, some people ask me when I am going to really retire. I tell them when my associate Darrell's son Jack is ready to take over. He is only four-years old, so that should tell you something!.

NINE
Using Your Policies as Your Future Operating Account

I am going to start by reminding you to keep an open mind. Try to forget all your previous ideas about life insurance and that I am an insurance agent. Try to remain logical as this could enable you accept a different way of looking at life insurance.

I found out early in my career that life insurance was not one of the easiest things to sell, due in no small way to the negative aspects that are normally associated with it—particularly its association with death. I realized that the positive side had to be presented in such a manner that prospective clients would be seeking *me* out, rather than the reverse. I wanted these clients to see that what I was offering was not just security for the future but also prospects for the present.

Let me see if, by asking you a few questions, I can get you to seriously consider life insurance:

1. If you save $10, $100, $1,000, $10,000 or $100,000 in the bank, is the interest taxable? *Yes.*
2. If you save $10, $100, $1,000, $10,000 or $100,000 in a life insurance policy, do you pay tax? *No.*
3. Where should you save your money?

I do not object to paying income tax on income, but I do not want to pay income tax on savings. I find it difficult to believe that there is anyone who would pay tax on their savings when there is an alternative. Surely, "in a life insurance policy" would be the logical answer to the third question. (Especially in view of the first-year cash value products now available through life insurance companies.)

Unfortunately, most agents do not market life insurance as a method of tax-free savings. They prefer to approach clients with "protection." Do not misunderstand me; protection is a very important part of life insurance, but it is not the sole reason that one should consider when purchasing of life insurance.

Statistically, a person does not require life insurance because, statistically, most people live long enough to raise their family, pay off their mortgage, enjoy some luxuries in life, and save enough to retire comfortably. However; if the statistics are 99 per cent in favour of a long life, but you, unfortunately, turned out to be in the 1 per cent, I rather doubt if statistics would mean very much to you. Theories of probability and possibility mean very little to a family where a bereavement has brought not only sorrow but also despair. Nevertheless, statistics do indicate that your chances of living are better than your chances of dying at an early age—so why would you buy life insurance?

I believe that you should be purchasing permanent life insurance (also known as whole life insurance) for two reasons other than just protection: as a future tax-free savings account and to use as your future operating account.

There it is again—a future operating account. Let me explain what I mean by that: An operating account is the money you save and spend, or borrow and pay back.

Most people start out by using their chequing or savings account as their operating account, and they start out on a line of zero, working from paycheque to paycheque. To keep the numbers simple, let's assume that one person may have $100 in the account and $100 in debt:

In account	$100
Debt	(100)
Balance	0

Another person may have a balance of $599 in the account for emergencies:

In account	$500
Debt	(100)
Balance	$400

This person could then afford some small emergencies or expenditures.

A balance of $1,500 would be even better:

In account	$1,500
Debt	(100)
Balance	$1,400

Of course, this balance could be any amount with which you feel comfortable. Some people are quite content to have $500 in the bank, while others get paranoid if their balance is below $5,000. Only you can decide which sum you can live with without worry.

That figure is what I call your comfort zone. Your comfort zone should be a figure that can cover some of the unexpected things that can upset your budget.

If you decide that your comfort zone is $3,000 then you treat $3,000 as your line of zero bank balance. In other words, if your budget is up or down by $250 in a month then you will have a balance of $3,250 or $2,750 respectively, instead of $250 in the black or $250 in the red as would be the case with an actual zero balance.

This idea of a comfort zone allows you some flexibility. If your figure is $3,000, then you have $250 per month for the next twelve months for those unexpected items until it is time for you to rewrite the loan, at which time you top up your emergency account. Similarly, a comfort zone of $6,000 allows you a cover of $500 per month.

The account in which you maintain your comfort zone or emergency account is called your operating account. Many people use a daily-interest savings account as their operating account, in conjunction with a chequing account. All income goes into the operating account:

- salary;
- family allowance;
- interest income;
- tax rebate;
- rental income; and
- miscellaneous income.

Your budget for each month comes out of this account, and if there is a balance above your comfort zone then that balance could be applied against outstanding loans, or put into savings or investments.

Most people start out by borrowing and paying back—certainly for major purchases such as cars—but they are subject to the fluctuating interest rates charged by the various lending institutions.

Another type of person will not borrow except for a mortgage for a home. They save and spend; then save and spend again; then save and spend again! If they do not save then they cannot spend. If they do not save again then they cannot spend again.

The account operated by this second type of person is not an investment account, and it is not even a savings account. It is a temporary savings account, where you save only until you have enough to spend, and then you save until you can spend again. I am sure that most of us have, or have had, this type of account, and in general it earns very little in the way of interest—to say nothing of compound interest.

I'll show you how you can effectively earn compound interest on your operating account by using permanent life insurance policies as your future operating account.

Some types of operating accounts include:

Savings Account. Each time you make a withdrawal you lose the compound interest forever.

Bank Loan. You pay the principal and interest to the bank at its repayment terms.

Permanent Life Insurance Policies. You pay the principal and interest to yourself on your terms. In other words, you fix your repayment schedule to meet your own budget. Policy loans used to float 1–2 per cent below prime when prime was 8–10 per cent. Now that prime averages between 4 to 6 per cent London Life has fixed its rate at 8 per cent, which makes it more advantageous to use your policy as collateral for a line of credit at prime from a financial institution and is more convenient for day-to-day banking. Finally, of even greater benefit, the money you pay back is going back into your own tax-free savings account for future use.

So, which would you prefer? If you are still in doubt, read on.

The objective is to use your permanent life insurance policies as your operating account.

If your policies have a cash value of $10,000, $20,000, $30,000, $40,000 $50,000, then:

Where would be the logical place from which to borrow?
Where would be the logical place in which to save?

You save for future items by repaying the policy loans. In other words, pay back your total available cash flow into your own tax-free savings account (i.e. back into your own policies) for future borrowing.

In order to use a permanent life insurance policy as your future operating account, it is, of course, necessary to own one. The amount you can use from your policies is dependent upon how long the policies have been in force, and upon how much you have paid into them.

To many people, purchasing life insurance is low on the list of priorities that must come out of a paycheque. In many cases it is included only because the purchaser felt that the only way in which they could get rid of a persistent life insurance agent was to agree to purchase a policy— and the less one could get away with, the better. Even if what the agent was saying made a lot of sense, what they were talking about was always going to happen so some other person, not you. Many agents are in fact genuinely concerned at the potentially horrendous situation that could hit a family without adequate life insurance coverage.

Let me show you a way in which you can take care of your priorities and at the same time provide for your family.

First, would you agree:

- That to go on a $1,200 vacation each year you would have to set aside $100 per month and that if you used that $1,200 each year on that vacation then you would not earn much interest on the $1,200?
- That cars depreciate around $1,000 to $1,800 each year, depending upon the age and model of the car? If your car depreciates every year at an average of $1,800 per year then that is another $150 a month on which no interest is earned?

Then let me ask you:

- How many people do you know who pay $250 per month on life insurance? Very few.
- How many people do you know who pay $250 per month between their car and vacation payments, to say nothing of other payments? Almost everyone.

Stop for a moment and consider just how much you yourself spend each month on a car and vacation payments. I am suggesting that if you are paying out approximately $250 each month on these or similar items then you could (depending upon your own circumstances and requirements) be purchasing an excellent life insurance policy that would give you first-rate coverage, *and* provide you with a method of paying for your future cars and vacations (or whatever) with cash from your future operating account (i.e., with cash from your own policies). In fact, these figures are probably too conservative. There are many people who spend $2,500 to $5,000, or even more, on a vacation which translates to between $200 and $400 per month; and it is not uncommon for cars to depreciate $2,500 to $5,000 each year, which is another $200 to $400 a month.

Let's look at the upper limits in both of the previous items: $800 per month comes to $9,600, which is less than 25 per cent of a $40,000 income, and less than 20 per cent of a $50,000 income.

So not only is this product a future operating account, but also provides the security of life insurance coverage.

Borrowing for a major purchase such as a car is a good example. It is fair to say that, at least in our early years, the majority of us purchase our cars with a loan from a bank, credit union, or finance company. Given the option of paying a high interest rate to a lending institution or a line of credit at prime using your life insurance policies (read future operating account) where you are paying the principal and interest back to yourself, does not the latter method make more sense?

Of course it does! And this is why you should be purchasing permanent life insurance.

After I've explained this to people, they generally ask, "How much does all of this cost?" Most life insurance companies have what they call volume discount, based on a rate of $1,000 unit cost of life insurance coverage. The following table is an example of London Life's volume discount rate for a twenty-five-year-old male. Most other companies have similar discounts.

20 Pay Life Age Twenty-five (First-Year Cash Values)

Amount ($)	Annual ($)	Per $1,000
10,000	293	29.30
25,000	680	27.22
50,000	1,326	26.52
100,000	2,597	25.97
200,000	5,139	25.66
250,000	6,260	25.04

Using the figures in the table, if you wished to purchase a $10,000 20/Pay Life insurance policy (future operating account) it would cost $293.20 per year or $29.30 per $1,000, and you can see from the table that the unit price per $1,000 reduces as the coverage increases. Obviously, the larger your future operating account, the sooner you will be able to make use of it as your operating account.

However; in order to qualify for a rate of $25.04 per $1,000, which is $4.26 per $1,000 or 17 per cent cheaper than the $10,000 rate, you have to purchase a $250,000 20/Pay Life policy. This is great for me, as I am in the business of selling life insurance, and it could be great for your beneficiaries should anything happen to you, but what is in it for you, because, as you will remember, statistics indicate that it is going to be the other person who requires life insurance—not you.

I'll tell you what is in it for you: This is going to become your future operating account. This is what is going to allow you to become your own banker, your own loan officer—to control your own financial destiny!

Obviously the larger your future operating account, the sooner you can use it, and the more control you will have of your own life. Unfortunately, many people do not own large life insurance policies because they do not understand some of the basics of simple financing, but let me ask you: If money was no problem, would you purchase $250,000 of life insurance to use as your future operating account?

Most people I've asked have said they would, but coming up with that kind of money was a problem. To address this issue, London Life has a policy that lends itself perfectly to use as your operating account and Freedom 55 at the same time.

BOB'S COMMENTS: USING YOUR POLICIES

The new first-year cash value 20-Pay-Life policies make it much easier for the average person to create their own line of credit at the prime interest rate (as opposed to using a credit card, etc.) as soon as the end of the first year if you adopt my Formula for Success (minimum $10,000 premium or 25 per cent of your gross income). The reason I use $10,000 premium is that $10,000 represents 25 per cent of $40,000 gross income.

I agree that there is no way a young person can afford to pay a $10,000 premium from a $40,000 income, but there is no way they can buy a car or a house either without borrowing money.

There is nothing wrong with borrowing money especially if it is to purchase assets. Millionaires borrow money and the banks are in the business of lending money.

I must give the banks credit: They are the only lenders that care about your total debt. You can be at your total debt income ratio with a bank and the next day lease a car, get a credit card, and none of them care about your debt ratio. However, if you are going to use a bank you have to understand the lending criteria (illustration using $40,000 gross income):

$40,000 \times 12 = \$3,333$ per month
35 per cent net-debt ratio: $\$14,000 \times 12 = \$1,166$ (paying rent)
40 per cent gross-debt ratio: $\$16,000 \div 12 = \$1,333$ (own a home)

The other 60 or 65 per cent is for living expenses and income tax. The difference between 35 and 40 per cent is your living accommodation, and if your gross-debt ratio is less than 40 per cent, the bank considers your total debt to be safe.

At one time a bank would give a person a loan for major purchases repayable over five years if it fitted into their gross debt ratio.

A $40,000 loan payable over five years at 8 per cent (3 per cent over prime at time of writing) = $806 a month and every time you wished to rewrite your loan it meant paperwork.

The banks are now considering unsecured lines of credit at X, Y, or Z over prime, depending on your previous credit rating, with a 2 or 3 per cent repay depending on the bank.

$40,000 × 2 per cent repay = $800 (same as five-year loan)
$40,000 × 3 per cent repay = $1,200 (same as three-year loan)

Using $40,000 with 2 per cent repay ($800 per month, well under the net-debt ratio)

$40,000
$\underline{-10,000}$ premium,
first-year cash value $4,800
(same as saving $400 per month)
– Estate value $200,000, $300,000, $400,000
depending on age

$30,000
$\underline{-10,000}$ RRSP—tax rebate approx. $3,000 ÷ 12 = $250 per month
(Which you would not get if you did not borrow the money)
$20,000
$\underline{-10,000}$ Pay off credit card—saves $X a month

$10,000
$\underline{-10,000}$ GIC for emergencies, future down payment
0

Approximate Repay: $40,000

$ 800 25 per cent of gross
    250 tax rebate
    366 difference between 25–35 per cent debt ratio
$ 1,416
× 12
$16,992 principal
– 1,992 less approximate interest
$15,000 principal (objective to reduce principal by $15,000)

$15,000 principal
+10,000 GIC
$25,000 down payment on $100,000 house

$75,000 line of credit × 5% = $3,700 ÷ 12 = $313
         at prime × 6% = $4,500 ÷ 12 = $375

Policy second year:
first-year cash value $ 4,800
second-year increase   7,200
total $12,000

                           $12,000
to pay premium   10,000
                           $ 2,000   To pay interest

Situation second year:
Interest on $10,000 × 6% = $ 600 ÷ 12 = $ 50
House $75,000 × 6% = $4,500 ÷ 12 =   375
Loan   2% repay on $40,000 =   800
                                                $1,225

Well under gross debt ratio of $1,333

The next chapter shows you how, by understanding some simple financing, you can improve your lifestyle and standard of living.

TEN
Simple Financing

BOB'S COMMENTS:

Don't let all the figures in this chapter confuse you. Just accept the fact that it can be advantageous to borrow for certain items regardless of the interest—interest is the cost of doing business. This chapter also explains the Rule of 72, which is the rule of compounding interest.

Do you realize that if started your career at age twenty-five, retired at age fifty-five, then lived to age eighty-six that you will spend more years in retirement than you have worked? If that doesn't make you think about the future and adopt my Formula for Success and Formula for Freedom 55, I don't know what will.

I have complete confidence in the accuracy of the following statements:

Money costs money. If you borrow money, then you must pay interest to your bank, credit union, or finance company. There are few people lucky enough to have a loan without the penalty of paying interest.

That it can be better to borrow than to pay cash. This is a statement that many people have difficulty accepting for three good reasons: they don't like to pay the high interest rates that they would be charged by lending institutions; they do not want to be in debt; and they were raised to believe that it is wrong to borrow money.

I can appreciate the third point, as I am very familiar with it myself. It was one of the most difficult things for me to overcome in my own lifestyle. I was born and raised in Scotland in a social environment where if one could not afford to pay cash, then one did without! Debt was anathema and when combined with pride, plus a certain amount of superstition, it reached heights that appear ridiculous in this day and age. For example, I can clearly remember my mother, at a few minutes before midnight on a New Year's Eve, running upstairs to pay back her sister a small loan of tuppence ha'penny, which is less than five cents by today's comparison. It was critical to her that she enter the New Year absolutely free of debt.

That attitude may have been well and good in Scotland in the 1930s and 1940s when relatively few people could afford to own their own home and run a car. Nevertheless, it caused me no end of problems when I came to Canada in 1953 and discovered that it was not really practical to pay off one's mortgage on December 31, and then take out a new mortgage on January 1, all in order to enter a new year free of debt. But, I forgot, mortgages are different, aren't they?

No, they are not! In fact, they are just one more method of borrowing, and if the majority of us did not borrow for our homes then we would not end up owning one, or even the equity that a partially paid mortgage represents. Therefore, I am going to state once again: *It can be better to borrow than to pay cash.* At least for some things.

I never cease to be amazed by the way that many people will argue that something *cannot* be done, rather than ask how it *can* be done. I try to impress upon people that when someone tells them something that they do not agree with, they should not argue with that person, but instead ask them to explain their point of view. (Unfortunately, at times I have not taken my own advice.) By following my advice, you will then know all that you already knew, plus you will also know the point of view from which they would argue. Just because you know their views, it does not necessarily follow that you must accept them.

Therefore, when I say that "It can be better to borrow than to pay cash," and your immediate reaction is to disagree with me, just remember that someone told you, "Don't argue, just ask them to show you."

I am constantly surprised by the way some people refuse to open their minds enough to at least listen to new ideas. After all, it costs nothing to listen. If what you hear makes sense, then you can act on it if you wish, and if it does not make sense to you then you are free to reject it.

I am suggesting that you invest some of your time in the hope that you may learn something that may change your thinking about financing or about money in general. Let me show you an example using $1,000:

In order to purchase a $1,000 item with cash you must first have accumulated the $1,000. You could have accumulated the $1,000 in several ways perhaps over a few months. For the purpose of this example I am going to use 12 months. In brief, you have saved the money. You have purchased the item. You now have no money.

Consider this: You had to do without the item until you accumulated that first $1,000. The item for which you are saving may in fact cost more than $1,000 by the time the 12 months are up. Each time you brought your bank account back to zero you not only lost the interest on your $1,000 but also the interest on the interest.

This has become your "operating account." You saved and then you spent, you saved and then you spent, you saved and then you spent...If you did not save, then you could not spend. It is that simple!

This account should not be compared with an investment account. In fact, it should not even be compared with a savings account. It is a temporary savings account. Your money is saved in the account only until you are ready to spend it, and then you must save all over again.

What I plan to demonstrate to you is how you can effectively earn compound interest on your future operating account by using your permanent life insurance.

Using the earlier example of the $1,000, what happens when you borrow instead of paying cash is that you keep your own $1,000, which earns compound interest, and at the same time you pay simple interest on your loan.

At the end of the first month you have an asset of $1,000 plus interest, and your liability is $1,000 plus interest, minus repayment, and the gap between the two gets wider each month. Therefore, you're never in debt. In fact, you are in a position to pay off your liability at any time.

There is a difference in *having* a debt, and *being* in debt. You are not in debt, as so many people seem to think, if your assets equal your liabilities (this is a basic principle of accounting).

To show you that it can be better to borrow than to pay cash, I'll use an example using simple numbers albeit low numbers. A young couple, both twenty-two years old, are starting out in their married life with all the normal expectations: buy a nice home, raise a family, enjoy some of the luxuries of life, save enough to be able to retire comfortably, and leave a reasonable estate for their heirs. Before they start out on that particular road, however, they are determined to have a nice honeymoon, and for this they are prepared to spend $1,000 out of the $2,000 that they have saved in the year in which they were engaged.

I suggest that they would be better off if they borrowed the $1,000 for their honeymoon. This advice is contrary to everything that they had been taught, and their immediate reaction is that it cannot possibly be correct. On the other hand, they are young! They are smart! Smart enough not to argue but ask, "How?" I show them the first step in simple financing.

Registered Retirement Savings Plan (RRSP)

I tell them that if they borrowed money for their honeymoon, they could keep the $2,000 and put it into an RRSP, which would mean that they would have both a honeymoon and a $2,000 RRSP, instead of a honeymoon and $1,000 in the bank. (The reason I have used an RRSP in my first example is that it is tax deductible and the savings in tax is greater than any interest charges, which I shall show you in a later example.) The present basic rules for an RRSP can be found on page 56. For more advice on the subject you should speak to your life insurance agent, banker, stock broker, or your personal financial adviser.

Although the rules for RRSPs change from time to time, for the average person it is still one of the most legitimate methods of postponing income tax payments. I suggest that you delay contributing to an RRSP until you study the current RRSP rules and feel comfortable with the concept of basic financing.

For our young couple, the only alternative to using their own money is to borrow. Let's assume they can earn 10 per cent on their $1,000, which equals $100 yearly interest or $1,100 savings in the bank at the end of the year, and it is going to cost 13.5 per cent to borrow for their honeymoon. Most people would agree initially that there is no way in which one can earn 10 per cent and pay 13.5 per cent and come out ahead. Would you not be inclined to agree with that logic? Well, you would be wrong! This is where the lesson in simple financing almost begins and ends. I'll demonstrate how it can be better to borrow than pay cash by using some actual bank figures.

To borrow $1,000 at 13.5 per cent over twelve months:

Amount Borrowed	Nominal Rate	Monthly Payment	Total Loan	Interest on Loan or Cost of Loan	Effective Rate
$1,000	13.5%	$89.55	$1,074.60	$74.60	7.46%

In the bank the $1,000 earned our couple $100. This table shows that to borrow another $1,000 it cost them only $74.60 (i.e., 7.46 per cent). How did that happen when we had already agreed that you could not come out ahead by earning 10 per cent and paying 13.5 per cent? Here's how:

The $100 of interest was earned because the original $1,000 was left in the bank for the whole year. On the other hand, while their loan started off at $1,000, they reduced it each month, and paid interest only on the balance owing. In other words, they only owed the bank $1000, $900, $800, $700 etc., for 12 months, 11 months, 10 months, etc, respectively.

Have you ever heard of decreasing balance? I am sure you have, but I am just as sure that you rarely think about it. Why did my mother not tell me about decreasing balance? For the simple reason—she did not know! Because my mother never borrowed there was never any opportunity to find out that, certainly for some things, it "Can be better to borrow than pay cash."

Let's use that same table and plug in some other numbers:

Amount Borrowed	Nominal Rate	Monthly Payment	Total Loan	Interest on Loan or Cost of Loan	Effective Rate
$1,000	16.25%	$90.84	$1,090.88	$90.88	9.00%
$1,000	18%	91.68	1,100.16	100.16	10.01%
$1,000	18.25%	91.79	1,101.48	101.48	10.14%

From this we can see the following:
- If our young couple had to pay 16.25 per cent, then the cost would be $90.88, but as they earned $100, they would still be ahead.
- If they had to pay 18 per cent, then the cost would be $100.16, but they earned $100, so they break even.
- If they had to pay 18.25 per cent, then the cost would be $101.48— Oh, oh, they are over by $1.48.

What, then, does all this tell us? It tells us that it is not so much the interest rate that matters—it is the differential. As you can see from the example, you can afford to pay 8 per cent more than you earn and still break even. In other words, if you can earn more than the effective rate of interest then you can afford to pay the nominal rate, and the effective rate will hardly change even if the loan is carried over a three-, five-, or ten-year period. (You can check this out with your banker.) The effective rate is the total cost of your loan over the total period of the loan, and banks have to tell you the total cost of any loan under the new full-disclosure rules about lending centres.

Let me give you a couple of examples to clarify this point. In 1982 when Canada Savings Bonds were paying 19.5 per cent, all you had to do was to take the rate you could earn plus the 8 per cent differential, for a total of 27.5 per cent. (This is just an example. For differential on other percentages, see the Daryl Diamond Table on page 91.) This meant that you could pay as high as 27.5 per cent to borrow money, and still come out even. The highest rate the banks ever reached was about 23.5 per cent and you would never pay the highest interest rate on a fully secured loan (which you would have, because, like our young couple, you left your $1,000 in the bank).

If Canada Savings Bonds paid 12 per cent, then you would take the rate that you are earning, add on the 8 per cent, which means that you could afford to pay as high as 20 per cent in order to borrow money, and you would still come out even.

If the banks charge between 14 and 16 per cent on loans, their payment on savings would normally be approximately between 11 and 13 per cent. Nevertheless, it is still the differential that counts, not the rate. In fact, the differential figure increases to 10 per cent if the bank rates increase to 23 per cent, and to 11.5 per cent if the rates reach 26.5 per cent, so you can see that the figures are always related. By using between 6 and 8 per cent as your differential you should not go wrong.

If you remember, there is a saving of 17 per cent of the premium if you purchase a $250,000 future operating account rather than one for $10,000, because of volume discount. This means that you could pay as much as 23 to 25 per cent to break even if you were to borrow in order to purchase your future operating account.

Let's assume that the young couple did as I suggested, borrowed for their honeymoon and put their own money into an RRSP (which I know would normally be one of their last priorities at this stage of their life). What effect will this have on their goals?

By borrowing for their honeymoon and putting their own money into an RRSP, their tax saving will be much greater than any interest charge. You have already seen how you can pay 18 per cent, earn 10 per cent, and still come out even. Here's how you can effectively pay less than 18 per cent, earn more than 10 per cent, and come out ahead.

Daryl Diamond* Table

As rates of return and borrowing increase, our interest margin increases.

Interest Rate (%)	Loan Cost ($)	Return (%)	Allowable Spread (%)
16	88.77	9	7
17	94.46	9.5	7.5
18	100.16	10	8
19	105.88	10.5	8.5
20	111.61	11.25	8.75
21	117.31	11.75	9.25
22	123.13	12.5	9.5
23	128.92	13	10
24	134.72	13.5	10.5
25	140.53	14	11
26.5	149.28	15	11.5

*Daryl Diamond was a London Life who constructed this table for his clients' reference.

By purchasing an RRSP that was paying only 10 per cent, our couple would earn $100 interest; however, they would also qualify for a tax rebate. This would be $300 if they were in the 30 per cent tax bracket, $400 if in the 40 per cent bracket, and $500 if in the 50 per cent bracket. We'll assume that they are in the 30 per cent bracket and would therefore receive a tax rebate of $300; this could be applied directly against their loan, reducing the interest charges.

If the interest on $1,000 at 18 per cent was $100, then the interest on $700 at 18 per cent would be only $70, or an effective rate of 7 per cent, which is less than either 18 per cent or 10 per cent. This also means that although the $1,000 RRSP certificate cost only $700, the same RRSP certificate will still earn $100 interest. Extending this further, it means that the $700 investment earns $100, which is an effective 14 per cent return.

In 1982 the couple could have purchased Canada Savings Bonds at 19.5 per cent, which could be registered as an RRSP and would have earned $195 interest, so now the $700 (after tax rebate) would have earned $195, for an effective rate of better than 27 per cent. Is 27 per cent better than 10 per cent?

Do I need to go on with this example? It continues to improve as your tax bracket increases. For example, if you were in the 40 per cent bracket you would receive a tax rebate of $400; therefore, $600 would have earned $195 interest, and if you were in the 50 per cent bracket you would receive $500 rebate, and so $500 would earn $195 for an effective rate of 39 per cent.

It is worth remembering that young couples are usually in a higher tax bracket because normally they are both working and therefore cannot claim the marital deduction. This is all the more reason for them to invest in RRSPs while they are young.

BOB'S COMMENT:

Some people believe that a risky approach is best for young investors who have the time to gamble with their RRSP funds, whereas I maintain you don't need to gamble. Take the safe route and you will still have more than sufficient funds to provide for early retirement.

Once you have put money into an RRSP then no one can force you to take it out until your seventy-first birthday, at which time the government will tell you that you have sheltered this money from tax long enough, and you must start to draw it out and pay tax on it (see rules on RRSPs on page 56).

There is another advantage to contributing to RRSPs while young. Later on, because of the limit of contributions to RRSPs you may not be able to contribute as much on a personal basis due to your contributions to a company pension plan. You will find that $1,000 invested in an RRSP at age twenty-two is much better than $3,000 invested at age thirty.

This is where the Rule of 72 comes into play. It is a simple, arithmetical rule for compounding interest, and it works like this: divide 72 by the interest rate you can earn, and the result gives you the number of years it will take for money to double at that interest rate:

$72 \div 4\% = 18$ years
$72 \div 6\% = 12$ years
$72 \div 8\% = 9$ years
$72 \div 10\% = 7.2$ years
$72 \div 12\% = 6$ years
$72 \div 18\% = 4$ years

This is how the Rule of 72 applies to $1,000 at 18%:

```
           $1,000
  + 18%       180
           $1,180
  + 18%       212
           $1,392
  + 18%       250
           $1,642
  + 18%       295
           $1,937
```

However, if the interest is compounded every six months then the bottom line is almost $2,000—and these days one can compound monthly and even daily! The following example indicates $1,000 at 18 per cent with the interest compounded every six months:

```
              $1,000
  + interest      90
              $1,090
  + interest      98
              $1,188
  + interest     107
              $1,295
  + interest     117
              $1,412
  + interest     127
              $1,539
  + interest     139
              $1,678
  + interest     151
              $1,829
  + interest     165
              $1,994
```

So you can see that if the interest is compounded monthly or daily then the bottom line will be close to $2,000.

No one knows for sure what the interest rates will be like in Canada over the next several years: They are as likely to go up as down. I am more inclined to think that inflation alone will cause the safe, or lower, interest rate to increase. I hope that I am wrong, as high interest rates create at least two problems. Anyone borrowing money, even if that money is to purchase a home, has to pay that higher rate, and people who are already paying income tax on interest income end up paying even more in tax.

I would like to believe that our Canadian politicians and economists have found, or can find, the answer to controlling inflation, but that answer has not been found in Britain, Europe, or South America. However; if the inflation rate does slow down, then we will not require as much money for the future, and if the rate of inflation continues to climb then we will need the extra money in order to fight inflation.

So high interest rates can be terrible if they are working against you, but they are great if they are working for you; if you cannot beat inflation, then make inflation work for you.

In my next example I will use two rates to illustrate the Rule of 72: 12 and 18 per cent. Let us go back to our young couple again, and remember that the $1,000 that they put into an RRSP at age twenty-two was that same $1,000 which they had intended spending on a honeymoon. Let's see what would have happened to that first $1,000:

Age	18% Money Doubles Every 4 Years ($)	12% Money Doubles Every 6 Years ($)
22	1,000	1,000
26	2,000	n/a
28	n/a	2,000
30	4,000	n/a
34	8,000	4,000
38	16,000	n/a
40	n/a	8,000
42	32,000	n/a
46	64,000	16,000
50	128,000	n/a
52	n/a	32,000
54	256,000	n/a
58	512,000	64,000
62	1,024,000	n/a
64	n/a	128,000
66	2,048,000	n/a
70	4,096,000	256,000

Try applying the Rule of 72 to your own figures.

This next example shows the difference between putting $1,000 into an RRSP at age twenty-two and $3,000 at age thirty-four, at 12 per cent of interest (or in other words, where the money doubles every six years).

Age	$1,000 Starting at Age 22	$3,000 Starting at Age 30
22	$ 1,000	n/a
28	2,000	n/a
34	4,000	$ 3,000
40	8,000	6,000
46	16,000	12,000
52	32,000	24,000
58	64,000	48,000
64	128,000	96,000
70	256,000	192,000

Bear in mind that that $1,000 in an RRSP at age twenty-two represents the $1,000 that our young couple were going to spend on their honeymoon because they didn't want to borrow. Would you not agree with me that they would be better off if they borrowed for their honeymoon and put their own money in an RRSP?

In fact, if they, or any other young couple, followed my recommendation they could have borrowed for their honeymoon, put their own money in an RRSP, and then taken their $300 tax rebate and had a $1,300 honeymoon. Even if the $1,000 had been invested at 12 per cent, to have spent their cash on a honeymoon could have cost them more than $250,000 in lost RRSP savings.

My next question to the young couple is would they like to get an extra $1,500 back from income tax this year? If so, I then suggest that they borrow $5,000 to put into an RRSP. Assuming that their combined income was $25,000 to qualify under the contributions limits, and also assuming a 30 per cent tax bracket, they would receive a $1,500 tax rebate. This would represent $125 a month toward their bank loan—to say nothing of the fact that the $5,000 could be worth well over $1,000,000 by the time that they are seventy, even if the RRSP averaged only 12 per cent, meaning that money doubles every six years:

Age	RRSP Amount ($)
22	5,000
28	10,000
34	20,000
40	40,000
46	80,000
52	160,000
58	320,000
64	640,000
70	1,280,000

It seems almost too easy, doesn't it? Yet all I am suggesting is that young people put the maximum allowable contributions into an RRSP by using the cash-flow method of financing.

Would you like to retire early, or at least have the choice? Well, it does not just happen. You have to plan for it. Can you imagine what would happen to your RRSP if you were to make the maximum contributions every year for the next five, ten, fifteen, or twenty years, when that first $5,000 alone could be worth approximately $10,000,000 by today's normal retirement age if inflation takes interest rates up to 18 per cent?

In this era when both early retirement and job redundancy are becoming more commonplace, does it not make sense that you should be in control of your own financial destiny?

This is probably the appropriate time at which to decide just how much you should borrow and what size of future operating account you should consider. The next chapter addresses cash-flow financing where you learn what you should borrow for, and perhaps more importantly, what you should not borrow for, and also how much you should borrow.

ELEVEN
Cash-Flow Financing

In my opinion, cash-flow financing has to be one of the best ways of financing for the average person.

Your cash flow is your ability to save, spend, or repay. Eventually your mortgage payment will also become cash flow, unless you arrange a personal loan to cover your mortgage, in which case your mortgage or rent payments increase your cash flow immediately.

All you have to do is to understand the real meaning of cash flow.

Everyone has a cash flow. Everyone's cash flow is different. Everyone's priority for their cash flow is different.

You calculate your cash flow by adding together your net income and any other money that comes into the home each month, and deducting from that sum expenses like mortgage or rent, groceries, gas for the car or transit passes, telephone, utilities, pocket money, etc. Whatever is left is your cash flow, and it is from this amount that you pay for clothes, vacations, boats, insurance, etc. People who have a lot of monthly commitments and have a good credit rating can do a lot better if they understand the proper use of cash-flow financing.

Personal Cash-Flow Loans

Since the banks eased their regulations on personal loans based on cash flow and track record I have been able to help several young couples purchase their first house without any of them having to obtain a mortgage. In each case they had a personal loan instead of a mortgage, and this had several advantages, starting with the fact that their rent payments were

97

immediately converted to cash flow. However, there are other advantages to purchasing your home with a personal loan instead of a mortgage, and even personal loans have been superseded by powerline mortgages, home equity lines of credit, and other products (in other words, a personal line of credit using anywhere from 66 to 80 per cent of the appraised value of your home—more about home equity loans later).

With a mortgage, unless you are paying a higher interest rate in order to have life insurance on that mortgage, it is not paid off if you die. I am frequently surprised at the number of people who believe that their mortgage is paid off upon their death, as they distinctly remember some reference to insurance in the original legal documents when they purchased their home. More often than not, that reference to insurance was in regards to fire insurance, and was for protection of the mortgage company.

With a personal loan or line of credit or similar product, you do have to pay for the appraisal fee to verify that security, but you do not have an official mortgage on your home. If this type of loan had been available years ago, many people would not have lost their homes!

Ironically, as an inducement to get customers to share the risk with the bank the variable rate at the time of writing was lower than the fixed rate. An added factor is that in order to make the variable interest loans more attractive, it can be arranged for this type of loan to be insured so that if either the husband or the wife dies, there is no feeling of urgency to get the total paid off. Consequently, you can apply your total cash flow against the loan, knowing that you can always re-borrow this money by using your line of credit as your operating account.

With cash-flow financing you can save while you repay!

I doubt if you will find any cause to argue with the following points:

- Bankers will lend considerably more money to an established customer with a good credit rating than they will to a stranger who may have even more assets but who has no track record at the bank.
- It is easier to borrow money when you don't need to borrow than it is when you do.
- If you don't borrow when you don't need to, you may have difficulty getting the money when you do need it, and this is why you should establish a track record at the bank as early in your life as possible.

You should borrow only what you can comfortably repay, hence the reason for understanding cash flow and your potential line of credit.

There is a basic rule-of-thumb about borrowing. A banker will lend 100 per cent against liquidity because if you do not repay your loan then the banker can cash in your security. However, a banker will lend only 50 or 80 per cent against equity (depending on the type) because if you do not repay your loan then the bank would have to sell the security in order to get its money back. Unfortunately, most people borrow against equity: their house, car, boat, stocks, furnishings, personal effects. But, this is an area that the bank does not wish to get into. Bankers don't want your house or your car, they want your money; they aren't in the real estate or used-car business. This means that in some cases while you may have the equity to satisfy the loan it is really your cash flow that will be the measure of how you can service your loan. This is why it is important to have a good track record in handling your loans. Bankers are more concerned about the manner in which you service your loan than they are about your security because in today's money market the banks also have a cash-flow problem. They don't really want to see interest-only loans; they want to see action on the capital as well, in order that they can have the additional cash flow, which they can then extend to other customers and expand their operational base.

Banking has changed over the past few decades. At one time, banks would extend loans on a three- to five-year basis if they fitted into their net-debt and gross-debt criteria. The trouble with three- to five-year loans was that if you needed more money before the end of the term, it meant the loan had to be rewritten, which meant paperwork and time.

Nowadays, banks are considering unsecured lines of credit at 1, 2 or 3 per cent over prime depending on your previous credit history, with a 2 or 3 per cent repay, depending on the bank.

Your monthly payment is based on 2 or 3 per cent of the outstanding balance. The bank deducts the interest due and the balance is applied back on the amount available on the line of credit, and is reusable by borrowing to the limit available without requiring additional paperwork.

TWELVE
Some Points to Consider

For Parents and Grandparents

Think back to when you were in your thirties, forties, or fifties. Do you remember where you were living, how much you were earning, what your first house cost, and the price of a new car? How many times have you said to yourself that you wished you knew then what you know now?

Often I have clients ask me "Where were you ten years ago?" And I reply "You can't say that ten years from now." Yes! Things are different and I can only relate it back to my own circumstances.

Many of your children or grandchildren have very little debt when they get married, quite often the gifts they get from their wedding leave them debt free, at least for a while; but they are faced with purchasing a house, raising a family, cars, vacations, etc. which are of course much more expensive than when you got married.

I am sure that most of us, when we first married, were in similar circumstances. We owed a little bit on the car, a little bit on furniture, a little bit on the ring, and a little bit on the honeymoon, if you could afford one, and we tried to pay them off so that we could think about saving for a house.

I wish I knew then what I know now.

Using my own situation, I was earning less than $10,000 when I purchased my first $10,000 Life Premium to 65 policy at age thirty; and I can't remember just exactly how much I owed at that time but it could not have been much as it was hard to borrow any money when you were earning only $6,000 per year and still renting. Curiously enough, if the same rules for safe debt applied then, the safe debt ratio would be 35 per cent of gross (35 per cent of $6,000 equals $2,100 over 12 months is $175 a month). Yes, I could have purchased $100,000 Life Premium to 65 with a $1,544 ($15.44 per $1,000) premium to take advantage of the volume discount instead of the $10,000 with a $198.20 ($19.82 per $1,000) premium, which I did buy.

Yes, I could have purchased $100,000 if someone had taken the time to show me the future benefits.

Yes, I should have purchased $100,000 if I had known about my formula for success.

Yes, I would still have been borrowed up to the hilt in the early years, but it would have paid dividends today, which brings me to the point of selling policies on children and grandchildren.

Selling policies on children and grandchildren is often an easy sale because people love their children and sometimes the grandchildren even more. Grandparents are in a better financial position to purchase policies on their grandchildren than when they were able to purchase on their own children when they were younger. When I ask parents or grandparents if they are going to leave the children or grandchildren money in their will and if their answer is yes, I tell them to leave it inside a policy purchased on them when they were young and in good health and were not in a position to purchase life insurance themselves. Although these policies on children and grandchildren are in their names and on their lives, the parents and grandparents still own and control these policies to use as an operating account to help their children and grandchildren during the years the money is accumulating inside the policy. Remember, the criteria for purchasing life insurance is age and health: the sooner you buy, the better the return.

Why I Purchased Life Insurance for My Child

Richard Kemp, CFP, CLU, CH.F.C., Regional Director at Freedom 55 Financial in St. Catharines, Ontario, shares his thoughts on why he purchased life insurance for his daughter:

My story starts in the early 1980s when my wife and I purchased a participating life insurance policy for our newborn daughter.

At the time, we encountered much criticism for this decision. Many friends and family felt it wasn't prudent to spend yearly premiums on life insurance, because juvenile deaths are unlikely, and the money could be used for investments.

Despite their objections, we purchased a $250,000 participating life insurance policy for our daughter. We knew it was the right decision, because permanent life insurance would allow us to save money to help our daughter with whatever the future might bring. What's more, unlike non-registered investments, her participating policy accumulates cash value on a tax-advantaged basis, within limits.

Having the option to access the policy's cash value has come in handy through the years. For example, life insurance helped pay for our daughter's first car, university vacations, and her competitive basketball team and their travels. Her basketball skills helped her land a university scholarship, which led to a stint with a professional European basketball team. We used her policy's cash value to pay for the lodgings overseas, as well as flights home at Christmas.

Purchasing juvenile life insurance also allowed us to protect our child's insurability. At the age of 16, our daughter developed a heart murmur. Since she was already insured as a child, her policy guaranteed her insurability as an adult without a medical report.

When our daughter turned twenty-six, we transferred the life insurance policy to her. At that point, the death benefit had grown to $650,000, with a policy cash value of $80,000.

If she maintains the policy and pays back the policy loans, at the age of sixty her policy could have a $2.2 million death benefit and a $1 million cash value, based on the current dividend scale. That's incredible value, especially when you consider her premiums will remain unchanged at $1,600 per year.

While working as financial security advisers, my wife and I sold numerous juvenile life insurance policies to our clients. Based on our experiences, we wouldn't recommend anything less. Life insurance is a great way for new parents and grandparents to help give their children and grandchildren a sound financial footing.

Some Points to Consider

- Cash-flow financing is one of the most effective ways for the average person to operate his or her financing.
- If you apply your total cash flow to your personal line of credit, you will usually find that it will provide you with sufficient cash—and probably much more than you dreamed possible—to take advantage of opportunities as they arise.

- By listing your assets and your liabilities on a regular basis, you can keep an eye on your estate net worth and your liquid net worth.

This method usually accomplishes most people's basic desires, such as paying off their home, enjoying some luxuries in life, providing for their families in event of a premature death, and providing for a comfortable retirement much more easily and sooner than they had thought.

By changing your mortgage to a personal loan or line of credit, you give yourself much more flexibility as you can use 80 per cent of your home's appraised value as security. If your house is the sole security for this line of credit, then the loan is called a collateral mortgage loan, but there is no mortgage on your home as long as you continue to make the necessary payments on the loan; however, you do have to pay for the initial appraisal on your home. It is worthwhile to establish your credit at the bank regardless of whether or not you may need it in the future.

You will find that a good banker is an invaluable asset. Never let your banker down, and remember that protecting your credit at all times is of prime importance.

The extra liquidity created by your loan will allow you to make payments of your loan in an emergency or to purchase other assets.

If you follow certain rules, this system will perpetuate itself. So much depends upon just what you want to accomplish.

The amount of money that you are able to borrow in the future is based mainly on serviceability, which is your ability to repay; hence the reason for repaying your loan by paying as much as you can as opposed to paying only the amount required. This serves two purposes: You pay less interest and you increase your potential line of credit.

Banks are in the business of lending money in order that they make money. Therefore, they like to lend to people who pay back at least what they promised, or more, each month. If you show them that you are one of these people, you'll be surprised at just how much bankers will do for you once they know you.

Learn how to use amortization tables until such time as you may qualify for an interest-only loan or line of credit. For example:

Approx Monthly Payment ($)	Amount of Loan ($)	Rate (%)	Over Years
$1,200	50,000	15	5
$1,225	75,000	15	10
$1,300	100,000	15	25

If you were paying $1,200 per month on a loan of $50,000, depending on your security, you could have the use of another $25,000 for another $25 per month, or the use of another $50,000 for another $100 each month. You will find that bankers will consider different amortization periods for different types of purchases and in particular for appreciating assets. The following are some examples using a cash flow of $300 per month:

Amount ($)	Reason	Length of Time (years)	Monthly Cash Flow ($)
3,500	RRSP	1	300
9,000	Used car	3	298
13,000	New car	5	289
21,000	Personal loan	10	301
28,000	Real estate	25	294
30,000	Business or investment	Interest only	300

This will give you an idea of how banks look at security and service-ability on collateral loans in order to assist you when preparing a presentation. Using the above example, I don't know why anyone would drive a used car for $9,000 when they could drive a $13,000 new car for the same monthly payment; however, there is a gradual swing away from collateral loans to interest-only lines of credit that allow much more flexibility—providing you qualify.

I would suggest that anyone who has more than 25 to 33 per cent equity in their home should convert their mortgage to a line of credit, whether they require the additional funds at this time or not. By applying for a maximum line of credit based on 66 to 80 per cent of the appraised value of your home, and provided that you have the necessary debt service qualifications, the money is pre-arranged and there is nothing to pay, other than the appraisal and legal fees to register the security, until the funds are used. You will then realize that any extra money still available on your line of credit may be used to purchase other appreciating assets, such as maximum RRSP contributions each year. On the subject of appreciating assets, there is probably no finer, worry- and maintenance-free, appreciating asset than a permanent life insurance policy; especially if you consider prepaying the premiums or using the premium offset method of purchasing—either way works in conjunction with the 20/Pay Life, First Year Cash Value product now available.

Value of Policy (If Premium Offset Is Elected)

Year	Cash Value ($)	Estate Value ($)	Approx. Annual Increase ($)
7	13,100	206,255	643
15	18,108	132,169	1,042
20	26,869	159,844	2,662
25	41,924	258,430	3,609
30	66,418	386,318	5,895
55	616,929	1,616,855	50,834

Total premiums $8,829 original deposit, or $1,688 × 7 years = $11,816.

There is another choice. Rather than elect premium offset, you can simply continue paying annual premiums, which makes a lot of sense when the eighth year annual increase (approximately $2,505 less the $1,688 premium) shows a return over premium of $817 tax free and is much better than putting $1,688 in the bank or bonds at 10 per cent earning $168.80 of interest, which is taxable. Or you can let the policy carry itself for the balance of the twenty years until no more premiums are required (see calculations below).

VALUE OF POLICY (7TH YEAR)

Estate Value   **Cash Value**
$206,255 $ 13,100

VALUE OF POLICY (20TH YEAR) (if premiums paid)
Estate Value   **Cash Value**
$601,007 $ 68,982

Less annual premiums
$1,688 × 13 years × average
10% compound interest   ($ 45,534)   ($ 45,534)
                      $555,473 $ 23,448

AUTHOR'S COMMENTS
Banking has changed over the past few decades. At one time, banks would extend loans on a three-to-five-year basis if they fitted into their net-debt and gross-debt criteria. The trouble with this was if you needed more money before the end of the term, it meant the loan had to be rewritten, which meant more paper work and time.

Nowadays banks are considering unsecured lines of credit at 1, 2, or 3 per cent over prime depending on your previous credit history, with a 2 or 3 per cent repay depending on the bank.

Your monthly payment is based on 2 or 3 per cent of the outstanding balance. The bank deducts the interest due and the balance is applied back on the amount available on the line of credit and is re-usable by writing a cheque up to the limit available without requiring additional paperwork.

THIRTEEN

Life Insurance and the Prospective Purchaser

BOB'S COMMENTS

This is probably one of the best chapters covering general knowledge about the purchase of life insurance. Some of the figures and terminology have changed over the years but the facts are mainly based on pure logic and common sense.

When you consider purchasing life insurance, keep the following points in mind:

- concept
- pick your agent as you would your doctor
- basic types of life insurance
- points about price
- net worth
- planning
- return on investment
- advisers
- pitfalls of buying term and investing the difference
- points about competition
- inflation

Concepts

The main reason for buying insurance while you are young is that you can take advantage of the low premiums. Look at the following tables:

Class 1 (Non-Smoker)

Age	Yearly Premium ($)	Total Premiums to Age 65 ($)	Total Return at Age 65 ($)
25	1,095	43,800	393,644
26	1,132	45,280	369,712
27	1,171	46,840	347,153
28	1,212	48,480	325,828
29	1,256	50,240	305,956
30	1,301	52,040	286,861

Class II (Smoker)

Age	Yearly Premium ($)	Total Premiums to Age 65 ($)	Total Return at Age 65 ($)
25	1,379	55,160	451,451
26	1,427	57,120	425,047
27	1,478	59,120	399,880
28	1,532	61,280	376,136
29	1,589	63,560	353,614
30	1,650	66,000	332,523

Although the dividend scale may change through the years, the relationship of the increase in premiums and decrease in return with age does not change.

Consider three people: the first is twenty-five, the second is twenty-seven, and the third is thirty. Each of them buys an identical house, identical stocks, bonds, mutual funds, an identical new car, and checks their interest at the bank. What is the common factor? Each pays or receives exactly the same, regardless of age.

On the other hand, with life insurance, age is a governing factor—the older you are, the more expensive it becomes and the returns are less.

Bearing this in mind, if you are planning to buy a home, stocks, bonds, funds, a car, and life insurance, at some time in the future doesn't it make sense to buy life insurance first?

Pick Your Agent as You Would Your Doctor

You should choose your life insurance agent as carefully as you would choose your doctor, lawyer, or accountant. Try to find one in whom you can confide; one who will take the time to explain the nuances of life insurance and who will take the time each year or two to review your program in order to make certain that it is keeping pace with your changing needs.

You will probably find that life insurance is not as complex as you might have thought if you sit down with your agent and analyze how life insurance works in conjunction with what you want life insurance to do for you and your family.

As most company rates are comparable, there is really little difference between the life insurance companies other than the quality of the individual agent. This then leaves you completely free to use the agent of your choice, but I recommend that you talk with two or three before you decide.

If your agent is a member of the Life Underwriters Association of Canada, he or she comes under the rules of the Life Underwriters' Ethics and Practice regulations. If agents have their Chartered Life Underwriter (CLU) designation, this usually indicates that they have had several years in the life insurance business and have taken extension courses to improve their knowledge; therefore, they will be able to give you the benefit of that additional knowledge.

Basic Types of Life Insurance

There are many life insurance products on the market today, which sometimes confuses agents, let alone the general public. A few examples are:
- non-smokers' term
- current interest products
- universal life
- term to 100
- variable life
- adjustable life
- flexible premium life
- indexed life
- contingent life
- modified
- irreplaceable
- fixed increase
- last survivor
- term with annuity

Then, of course, there are all the old plans that were around when I first started in the insurance business and some of which are still around today:

- five-, ten-, fifteen-, and twenty-year terms;
- term to fifty-five, to sixty-five, to seventy;
- whole or ordinary life;
- limited pay; and
- endowments (which have become less popular).

The first thing that you should take into consideration is that all life insurance policies are calculated actuarially; therefore, the cost can be perceived in different ways. Some people say that term insurance saves you money because it is cheap whereas others maintain that it is cheap because it does not save money for you. Life insurance is usually the only place in which a person can save money, therefore; he or she would rather have a permanent plan.

I'll explain the basic differences, because all plans are a variation of a combination of insurance and investment.

Term Insurance

Term is like car or fire insurance. If you do not have a claim, then you do not get any money back. Term insurance gives you coverage for a specific period. This could be for one, five, ten, or fifteen years, or it could be to age sixty, sixty-five, or seventy, etc.

However, you should keep in mind that the premium increases each time the policy is renewed. For example, if you decide to purchase one-year term and to renew each year for a further year, then your premium would be increased each year. On the other hand, if you decide to purchase and renew in five-year segments, then your premium will be increased every five years. Then, again, you could buy term to age sixty-five or seventy, and this means that you pay the same premium up to that age, then your coverage ceases. You will find that although one-, five-, ten-year, etc., may be cheaper early on, the cost can become prohibitive in the later years when, statistically, you will need the coverage more.

That, then, is the basis for term insurance. You pay your money and you are insured for a specific period. If you have no claim, then you are out of pocket the money you have paid in premiums.

I compared term insurance to car insurance. How would you feel if you were offered car insurance at three times your present premium, but if you never had any accident or claim then you would get your money back?

Would you not at least be interested in hearing more about that proposal?

Unfortunately, you cannot buy car insurance in that manner, but you can buy life insurance like that. Many permanent life insurance policies, from the second, third or fourth year, will return the full premium in the form of tax-free savings inside the policy. Check that statement with your life insurance adviser.

Permanent Life Insurance

Permanent life insurance plans are all variations of whole life, as they are all calculated actuarially. Permanent plans include whole life; life premiums to ages fifty, fifty-five, sixty, sixty-five; ten-, twenty-, thirty-year pay life; and ten-, twenty-, thirty-year endowment.

More whole-life plans are sold than any other type, and in the opinion of many successful agents, whole life gives you the best value for your money, with the possible exception of the First-year Cash Value 20-Pay-Life policies, especially if you intend using your policies as your future operating account.

Points about Price

Have you ever stopped to think why it is that some people shop for price when they are purchasing life insurance, but disregard cost when it comes to buying a car or vacation package? I guess that it boils down to wants and needs; and I must admit that I believe that this is where the marketing of life insurance goes wrong. We appeal to the needs instead of the wants, whereas the car industry appeals to the wants.

For example, you need a car, and while a Cadillac will cost you much more than a compact, because you want a Cadillac you are prepared to pay whatever it costs. As either vehicle will transport you from point A to point B, it is obviously more than just a means of transportation you wish to have; therefore, to you, it would appear that it is worth the extra price to have what you want. Again, steak or lobster will normally cost you much more than hamburger or haddock, but you want that steak or that lobster, and you are prepared to pay the price for it, not just because it will satisfy your hunger—the hamburger or haddock would do that—but because to you it is worth the extra cost. This is called lifestyle.

When providing group insurance for their employees, many companies consider only the cost to the company in dollars and cents, and consequently cut corners and accept less than they should for their employees. The goodwill that could have been achieved is often lost because the employees consider that their employer considered only the minimum benefits as their worth. Cheap plans have a way of turning out to be the most expensive in the long run.

Net Worth

The majority of people are better off than they think they are. Everyone should prepare a statement of net worth every year or at least every two or three years.

If your net worth increases each year, then you are heading in the right direction. The simplest formula for the calculation of net worth is:

assets − liabilities = net worth.

There are in fact two types of net worth that should be taken into consideration: liquid and estate.

Liquid Net Worth

Liquid net worth is the amount of money you would have if you sold everything you owned, including your used toothbrush, and paid off everything you owed. The balance is your liquid net worth.

Estate Net Worth

Estate net worth is the market value of all your assets, plus the death benefit of your group and personal insurance, plus the death benefit of your pension plan, plus the total value of your RRSPs, minus your liabilities.

When you are calculating your estate net worth, you can place a higher value on your assets as they are worth more to you in terms of facility than the price you could expect to receive for them should you have to liquidate them.

There should be no need to lose any estate value through liquidation by a dependant if one has ensured that that dependant has been sufficiently provided for in the form of adequate life insurance on the death of a spouse or partner. If a widow received sufficient life insurance to pay off her mortgage and still be able to live in the style to which she had become accustomed, then she would not be in the position of being forced to sell off her house. There is nothing that says that a widow will receive a good price when selling a house. On the contrary, when potential purchases are aware that the house must be sold they normally lower their offer accordingly. Does not this reason alone justify you having adequate life insurance coverage in your estate?

Do you know what your liquid net worth and your estate net worth are today? The following table, with fictitious figures, may give you some idea of how to list your statement of both liquid and estate net worth.

Examples of Liquid Net Worth and Estate Net Worth

	Market Value	Liquid Net Worth	Estate Net Worth
Principal Residence	$50,000	$45,000	$55,000
Cottages, Condos, Lots	40,000	35,000	50,000
Vehicles	5,000	2,500	7,000
Personal Effects (percentages could vary)			
Clothes 10%			
Furniture 30%			25,000
Appliances 50%	10,000	5,000	
Bonds	5,000	5,000	5,000
Stocks, Gold, etc.	5,000	?	?
Group Insurance	0	0	50,000
Personal Insurance	0	2,500	102,000
Cash on Hand	1,000	1,000	1,000
	116,000	$96,000	$295,000
		+ value of stock	+ value of stock

(Replacement value if forced to sell)

Capital Gain Considerations*

	Original Purchase Price	Market Value ($)	Liquidated Value ($)	Estate Value ($)
Principal Residence	30,000	50,000	$45,000	55,000
Cottage	20,000	40,000	27,500	50,000

* The rules for capital gains are constantly changing, but these figures will give you some guidelines for establishing your liquid and estate net worth.

I have touched upon only a few general areas, and have made a few assumptions. You will see from the table that, if your house had to be sold, the seller may not receive full market value. If you had sufficient life insurance, however, your family would be in a position to wait for the best price, and if they didn't want to sell, regardless of price, then the real value to your estate would be the undefined value of allowing your family their right to maintain their current lifestyle in the same home, school, and community.

If the cottage had to be sold, then that sale could easily trigger a capital gain. With a vehicle, the estate value is the replacement value. The greater part of personal effects and furnishings generally have little in the way of real commercial value—the greatest value in these items is their sentimentality or their use to your survivors.

Items such as stocks and gold are, of course, always subject to market fluctuation. So, since you aren't likely to check the position of the market before you die, remember that an investment is an estate value only if you do not or cannot use the investment while you are alive.

I strongly recommend that you take an hour or two and estimate the value of both your liquid net worth and your estate net worth today, keep track of these figures for the next few years, and do some planning.

Planning

I have paraphrased the following material from an old London Life publication:

If You Died Tomorrow, Would Your Affairs Be in the Shape You Want Them to be In?

Would your spouse know where to find important papers? Would he/she have an adequate income? Would he/she know where to turn for advice? Perhaps the first step is to turn off the TV for an evening. Sit down with your spouse and talk not about a bigger TV or a new car, but about the future of your family. Talk about your plans for retirement. Have you started a savings fund? What monthly income will you have at age sixty-five? Talk about your plans for educating your children. Are you setting money aside? Will you have enough? Talk about your family's future if one or both of you should die. Do you have enough life insurance? If one of you is unemployed, would he/she have to find a job? Try to build a long-range financial plan for your family. If you already have one, analyze it for weak points, and decide how you can correct them.

Talk to the Specialists

Few people have the time or talent to do their own financial planning. That's why we have specialists: lawyers, life insurance representatives, trust officers, bankers. Seek them out.

Talk to a lawyer about wills. Both spouses should have a will. This guarantees that your money goes where you want it to go. Your lawyer can advise you on types of wills and ways of minimizing succession duties. One reason for each of you having a will is that you could both die in an accident. Include plans for guardianship of minor children and the management of their inheritance. Remember—your lawyer is a specialist.

Talk to a life insurance representative about a program that gives your family a regular income if you die. How much they would need depends on the size of your family, the size of your mortgage (if you have one) and your spouse's ability to work. A good life insurance representative will help you work out the details. He/she will recommend a plan tailored to your family's needs.

Talk to a banker, trust officer or investment dealer. Don't attempt to get rich overnight on the basis of office gossip or "confidential" tips. Talk to a person who knows the investment field. Explain your present situation and savings objectives. That person has the training and experience to give you sound advice.

Clean Out the Drawers

When you have taken care of wills, life insurance, investments and so on, put all the important papers where they will be safe and accessible. London Life recommends two places: a safety deposit box for your deeds to property, certificates for stocks and bonds, and valuable personal papers; and a private-papers box at home for everything your spouse needs in an emergency, for example, all insurance policies, wills, back–income tax returns, bank statements, marriage license, pre-nuptial agreements, and birth certificates.

Write a letter of agreement with your spouse. Summarize the program you have agreed on, the amount of insurance you each own, and how you would each like the other to carry out the program you have made. Each of you should include a record of your assets and liabilities. List the location of safety deposit boxes (and their contents) and all bank accounts.

List the names, addresses, and telephone numbers of your lawyer, life insurance representative, and a close friend who would help your spouse settle the affairs.

Talk to Your Spouse

Spend another quiet evening going over all the steps you have taken. Discuss life insurance, retirement, investments, wills, and so on. Go over the letter you have written and make sure you both understand it. You will both feel better when you have set your affairs in order. The time it takes is a small investment when you think of the tangled mess you might leave behind.

No one really appreciates the value of a good life insurance program until they have reason to call on it for some specific purpose in the future. This could be for protection, collateral, everyday cash, an operating account, or, eventually, to supplement retirement income.

Now is the time to talk about these things!

Return on Investment

What do you feel is a fair return on a fairly safe or guaranteed investment? Is that figure before or after tax?

Decide what rate of interest you can earn, and which tax bracket you will be in during the accumulation years. You will find that you cannot earn the higher interest rate and remain in the lower tax bracket. As your earned income increases and your investment income increases from accumulation, so does your tax bracket, lowering your net interest after tax.

It is usually compound interest (i.e., interest on interest) over the years that makes investments in bonds, term deposits, etc. appear to be better investments than putting the same amount of money in life insurance, and that is certainly the case in the early years; however, in order to earn compound interest on an investment, you cannot use that money for any reason—even if your roof falls in, your children are sick, or your car breaks down—without upsetting the compounding factor.

In my experience, the majority of young couples who are raising a family, buying a home, and so on, do not have money that they can do without in the early years, and therefore cannot take advantage of compound interest over a long period of years.

Net Interest after Tax

Before-Tax	Marginal Tax Bracket (%)									
	20	25	30	35	40	45	50	55	60	65
Return (%)	Net Interest after Tax									
6	4.8	4.5	4.2	3.9	3.6	3.3	3.0	2.7	2.4	2.1
7	5.6	5.3	4.9	4.6	4.2	3.9	3.5	3.2	2.8	2.5
8	6.4	6.0	5.6	5.2	4.8	4.4	4.0	3.6	3.2	2.8
9	7.2	6.8	6.3	5.9	5.4	5.0	4.5	4.1	3.6	3.2
10	8	7.5	7.0	6.5	6.0	5.5	5.0	4.5	4.0	3.5
11	8.8	8.3	7.7	7.2	6.6	6.1	5.5	5.0	4.4	3.9
12	9.6	9.0	8.4	7.8	7.2	6.6	6.0	5.4	4.8	4.2
13	10.4	9.8	9.1	8.5	7.8	7.2	6.5	5.9	5.2	4.6
14	11.2	10.5	9.8	9.1	8.4	7.7	7.0	6.3	5.6	4.9
15	12.0	11.3	10.5	9.8	9.0	8.3	7.5	6.8	6.0	5.3
16	13.8	12.0	11.2	10.4	9.6	8.8	8.0	7.2	6.4	5.6
17	14.6	12.8	11.9	11.1	10.2	9.4	8.5	7.7	6.8	6.0

Life insurance is a completely different form of investing from the one involving the compounding of interest. Life insurance should be bought with the thought of making use of it while you are alive in the form of collateral, emergency cash, early retirement, etc. Remember that an investment is an estate value only if you do not or cannot use it, now think of your life insurance as your operating account.

You will usually find that the major part of the average person's estate is their home and their life insurance. Neither was bought as an investment. The home was bought as a place to live, and the insurance was bought for protection. In many cases these turn out to be the best, or the only, investments ever made.

Advisers

You will come across advisers who advocate that you should buy term insurance and invest the difference, and the first place in which they recommend that you invest is in maximizing your RRSP contribution. I contend that this is a major contradiction. Think it out for yourself. To buy term insurance suggests to me that you anticipate dying before retirement. To buy maximum RRSPs suggests to me that you anticipate living beyond retirement. What you are doing is setting aside money for retirement, and at the same time betting that you are going to die before retirement. Does that make sense to you?

Any adviser who recommends this loses credibility with me. At least these advisers are admitting that there is a need for life insurance, so it is really not life insurance that is in question, just the type. In my opinion term insurance is the wrong type to buy. More claims are paid out on permanent insurance than on term. Unless one has a claim within the term, be it a five-, ten-, twenty-year term, or a term to age sixty, sixty-five, or seventy, that term insurance is only a cost. Term plans are calculated actuarially to be out of benefit before you die. If they were not, then insurance companies would have to increase their premiums. Term insurance is similar to buying a block of ice on time payments—by the time you get it all paid for, it is all gone! Term insurance saves you money because it is cheap? Wrong! It is cheap because it does not save money for you.

On the other hand, if you buy permanent life insurance, you can borrow and pay back, borrow and pay back, as often as you want during the years, without upsetting the final figures. In effect, you can earn compound interest on an operating account. Your policies act as your tax-free savings and operating account. This point is missed by many people.

In later years, you can borrow your RRSP contributions from the cash value of the policies and apply the tax savings to the loan along with your normal cash flow.

There may be a time when you face an interest income problem. This is when you should consider repaying your policy loans, because if you make maximum contributions to an RRSP each year, even though you have to pay income tax when you withdraw them, you will still be paying tax on interest income. This is the time to consider repaying policy loans and is why I believe that buying permanent life insurance as well as investing in an RRSP makes an excellent combination.

Pitfalls of Buying Term and Investing the Difference

As I mentioned, many advisers suggest buying term and investing the difference. However, some people who buy term never actually get around to investing; rather they spend the difference. Then again there are actually smart business and professional people who buy term insurance on advice given by their accountants, lawyers, and other would-be advisers instead of doing their own research.

Many articles that advocate buying term insurance also recommend being sure that the term is convertible. Surely as age is a major factor in purchasing life insurance, that if you are considering converting in the future, it would make more sense (and would be much cheaper) to convert sooner than later. Term insurance should be purchased only when there is a cash-flow problem. You cannot solve a permanent problem with temporary coverage.

A cold, but nevertheless realistic fact, is that the only way to win with term insurance is to die before your statistically allotted time. Think of term insurance as betting against the track, with the life insurance company being the track. If the track (or in this case, the life insurance company) was losing money, they would simply increase the premiums, whereas the reverse is happening—term policies are getting cheaper. Does that not tell you something?

If you buy permanent insurance the cost is the interest on the premium, because every dollar in excess of the interest on a fully secured loan is total principal on the loan, and is re-usable or re-spendable by you. If you compare even the cheapest term policies with the interest on the permanent premium you'll find that in most cases the interest is lower than the term-insurance premium.

My clients do not buy term insurance. They cannot afford it!

Many people who require a substantial amount of coverage often have a line of credit and have no trouble borrowing for permanent life insurance. If a bank will lend you money for articles that depreciate (cars, furniture, etc.), they will certainly lend you money to purchase life insurance, which appreciates and is classed as a good security by the bank.

Points about Competition

Many agents and brokers advocate that people cash in old permanent insurance plans to purchase some of the fancier new products. If these policyholders stopped to think, they would realize that there is no way in which an old policy can be replaced to their benefit. Each policy has to support itself actuarially, and a life insurance company cannot afford to pay the death benefits as they fall due if it has not earned enough money to pay the claim.

However, if your circumstances have changed since you originally took out the policy, and you feel that a better type of coverage would now be more suitable, I recommend that you make the change with the original company. Most firms realize that needs change, and they respond by revising the old policies to meet new needs—giving full credit for premiums paid to the initial contract.

If your agent advises changing an old contract that you have with another company, make sure that you get a quote for the new coverage from the original company before you make a decision to change. There are many agents who change companies for various reasons, and I have no axe to grind with them when they sell new insurance with their new company to their old clients. On the other hand, I am strongly opposed to agents who recommend replacing old insurance with new insurance in their new company. In most cases the client will never come out ahead. If the change is as good as they suggest then the logical recommendation, which should be for the benefit of the client and not that of the agent, would be to make the change with the client's original company.

A few agents even recommend replacing policies that they themselves have sold to a client while employed by another company. As that recommendation almost invariably involves replacing the policy with one purchased through the agent's new company, it is obvious that the agent is going to collect commission on the replacement, even though he also collected commission on the original policy when he made the sale to you. An agent earns his livelihood from the commissions on his sales, but it seems reprehensible for an agent to attempt to earn commission twice on a policy. This would be a case where you should consider replacing agents rather than replacing policies.

In the event of your untimely death, your family would soon realize that even the worst insurance plan was better than none at all, so whatever proposals you may be considering, please ensure that you are insured at all times.

Be cautious of agents who are recommending replacement.

Inflation

High interest rates are great if they are working for you, but absolutely dreadful if they are working against you. What I say is, if you cannot beat inflation, why not join it?

If I told you that life insurance is a great inflation fighter, you would probably accuse me of being biased because I sell life insurance. Consider the following example of purchases of $100,000 permanent life insurance, all purchased at age twenty-five. The first was bought in 1971, the second in 1981, the third and fourth are the smoker and non-smoker rates in 1986 using dividends to purchase paid-up additions in all cases.

Year	Premium ($)	Cash Value ($)	Total Cash Value + Paid-up Additions at 65	Estate Value ($)
1971	1,362	56,000	136,000	218,000
1981	1,311	56,000	343,000	543,000
1986	1,095	47,500	393,000	804,000
1986	1,379	54,000	452,000	785,000

(non-smoker) (smoker)

Can you tell me of any other product over the past fifteen years where the price has come down and the product improved? Well, yes, there is at least one. Computers have become much cheaper, and they have improved enormously. But why has life insurance improved? The reason is perfectly simple.

What were insurance companies charging for mortgages twenty years ago? Six per cent. What are they charging now? They are charging the going rate. What were insurance companies charging for policy loans twenty years ago? Six per cent. What are they charging now? They are charging the going rate. This means an increase in the company profits, which are distributed to policyholders in the form of dividends. As long as inflation increases, life insurance will continue to improve to keep pace with inflation, which is creating the increases.

So life insurance really is a great inflation fighter.

Have you ever thought of life insurance in that way before?

Other Points to Consider

- In the case of your death your bank pays out what you saved. Your life insurance company pays out what you intended to save.
- If you are single and childless, prepare adequately for retirement as you will have to support yourself.

Few people realize the real value of a good insurance program until they have occasion to call on it for protection, collateral, emergency cash, mortgage redemption, education, business opportunity, or perhaps to supplement retirement income.

Even at a time of death in a family, creditors still expect to be paid. Your life insurance agent is the one who brings you money, plus a lot of free service.

You do not require a lawyer to make a claim on a life insurance policy. All you have to do is to contact your agent or the company. Remember, there is no charge for settling a claim.

FOURTEEN
Life Insurance and the Adviser

This chapter is written with advisers in mind, but clients may also find the information useful.

Many years ago Ken Wylie, an American marketing and communication consultant, spoke at one of our company conferences about the legacy of a life insurance agent:

> If you were to read in the paper tomorrow morning that a local businessman had died and left a legacy of $10,000,000 to be used for needy people in your hometown, to help widows pay off mortgages, and send children to university, everyone would be impressed. But no one gives much thought to the average insurance agent who starts selling life insurance at age thirty, and if he only sold $1,000,000 of new insurance each year until he retired at age sixty-five, would leave a legacy of $35,000,000, which would be paid to needy people in his hometown, to help widows pay off mortgages, and send children to university.
>
> What kind of legacy will you leave? How much total insurance have you put in force up to now, and how much more will you put in force before the end of your career?
>
> There are few other careers that give you the opportunity of doing as much good, and—when you can accept the fact the insurance you sell will be paid out long after you have passed on—the thought of leaving a legacy like this can take a lot of the negativity out of the job!

The topics covered in this chapter are as follows:
* seminar selling
* negativity

- inflation
- selling to friends
- selling to relatives
- replacement
- term insurance
- rated policies
- power phrases
- other points to consider

Seminar Selling

Any agent who isn't taking advantage of seminar selling is missing the boat. Seminars give you the opportunity to tell your story to a lot of people at one time. Agents can work as a team, each expounding on his or her area of expertise.

Seminars are non-compromising. People who attend them should feel free to participate or not. Experienced agents can run the seminars, and the less-experienced agents can spend time prospecting for people to attend.

If you stop to consider it, a young agent spends much of her time prospecting, but, because of her inexperience, her ratio of sales to prospects is normally quite low. However, two birds can be killed with one stone by making good use of seminars where, through the experience of the older agents, sales can be made to prospects who might otherwise have waffled if dealing with the inexperienced agent and at the same time the young agent can benefit from observing the experienced agent in action. If young advisers work closely with experienced advisers, they'll make better use of their time when searching for fresh prospects, and become experienced enough to then pass their knowledge on to the next group of new advisers.

Negativity

Life insurance has always been a negative type of business, and this is one of the main reasons that some agents do only a mediocre job at best. Many young advisers just cannot accept the rejection and so there is a high turnover rate.

Many people have difficulty talking about death, disability, and old age, and will do anything to avoid discussing them, including being downright rude to insurance agents. That attitude, while being easy to understand, is also difficult to accept, and is one of the reasons so many advisers stop selling as soon as they can live within their income. Who needs to take any more negativeness?

It is essential to remember is that it is not *you* personally that these people are rejecting but the subject you will inevitably raise. You are going to ask them to face up to their responsibilities, point out that they could die prematurely and leave their family totally unprovided for, or that unless they prepare for retirement now, they could face a very bleak future. They are probably aware of all these facts, but, right at this moment they feel that they just don't have any spare money to put toward such events.

I prefer to emphasize the living benefits of life insurance rather let people believe that life insurance is a necessary evil. For instance, I firmly believe in the collateral value, and I demonstrate that aspect, along with how policies can be used as a future operating account (see page 149).

Inflation

Families cannot ignore the importance of life insurance in planning their future protection. Those who have already taken steps in the right direction should be reminded that protection that was adequate a few years ago probably will be insufficient for the future. It is your responsibility as a life insurance agent to ensure that your clients are adequately covered for the future—even if they think that today's needs are covered.

Demonstrate to them how life insurance is one of the few things that has not soared in price, and how it helps them to keep pace with inflation.

Show your clients how they can increase their coverage by using the paid-up additions dividend option, and how the level premium becomes easier to find over the years, either by increased income or by the deflation of the value of the dollar. Who can complain about buying more protection with cheaper dollars?

Established agents have many clients with programs that have been eroded by inflation. One of your major goals should be to ensure that these programs are updated. I have never heard of anyone complaining that they were left too much insurance, and I have never heard of anyone refusing the proceeds!

Inflation means that your client's present insurance program is no longer capable of doing its intended job. You should re-evaluate your client's coverage at least every five years in light of inflation.

BOB'S COMMENTS

If a young adviser, young prospect or anyone for that matter, was to follow my formula for success they will find that the formula will provide adequately for inflation in the future.

Selling to Friends

It can be embarrassing to discuss life insurance with friends, but wouldn't it be more embarrassing to tell your deceased friend's spouse that you never raised the subject because you didn't want to exploit your friendship?

Selling to Family and Relatives

Quite often this can be your most difficult sale. The family and relatives of life insurance agents sometimes do not receive the attention and service that they should, because other agents assume that you have spoken to them. This is also the case with neighbours and friends. It is up to you!

Replacement

Make use of your company's policy change department. You will be pleasantly surprised by what they can do to improve or upgrade old policies. There are very few cases where the replacement of old insurance is better than a policy change. Any replacement that is deemed necessary should be done through the original writing company. Even if the client's circumstances have changed since the original writing of the policy and you feel that a different type of coverage would be more suitable, it's still advisable to have the change made by the original writing company. Most company policy change departments are capable of revising old policies to meet the new needs, giving the client full credit for premiums paid to the initial contract. By doing this, you will gain the client's respect and perhaps future business, as well as potential references.

Term Insurance

Clients and agents who argue that term insurance is the best route to go, on the premise that you can purchase more coverage for your dollar than you can with permanent, are not always correct. Statistics show that many people are underinsured when they die, and life insurance agents are frequently blamed for selling $10,000 permanent instead of $100,000 term when the client needs the $100,000 coverage. If that was the choice then I would agree—the agent should sell the $100,000 term coverage. But what that agent should really have been trying to sell was the $100,000 permanent. This is one of the major reasons for me writing this book—how it is possible for the average person to purchase permanent insurance instead of term insurance.

What many people forget is that term plans provide coverage for a specific number of years or until a certain age, and that most term plans lapse or run out of benefit while the insured person is still alive because two out of every three adults live beyond age sixty-five. By that time, the term premium is usually too prohibitive to renew or convert.

Buyers and sellers of term insurance contribute heavily to people being underinsured when they die; the same term insurance that these buyers and sellers advocate is the main reason for not buying permanent insurance initially. Most term policies lapse when the premium keeps increasing. Term insurance is inexpensive when you are twenty-five, but the increase in premiums becomes prohibitive when you are forty, fifty, or sixty when it also becomes too expensive to convert. Statistics show that more claims are paid on permanent insurance than term insurance. Have you ever thought of it that way before? It is better to have a $10,000 or $25,000 permanent life insurance policy still in force at time of death than a $100,000 term policy that has lapsed or is out of benefit because you cannot afford to convert at a prohibitively high premium.

Rated Policies

A rated policy is a policy in which a life insurance applicant is charged a higher than standard premium to reflect a unique impairment, occupation, or health condition. I suggest that you refer to rated policies as standard policies for an older age. Many senior citizens are still quite healthy. Just because they are rated does not mean that they are expected to die soon. It just means that their chances are not quite as good as they would be if the reason for rating did not exist.

Bear in mind that while a rating can be reduced or removed, it can never be increased. In fact, if a policy is rated then the policy owner should consider purchasing additional insurance in case his condition deteriorates. If the rating is decreased or removed in the future, he should consider purchasing the total amount of life insurance that he think he'll require.

Keep in touch with clients who have rated policies. While the rating can be reduced or removed because of improved medical research or revision in health requirements, the change isn't carried out automatically. You, the client's agent, must apply have a rating reduced or removed, and only the client will know if there has been a significant improvement in the condition responsible for the rating being applied in the first place. This is an area where you can extend invaluable service to your clients.

Power Phrases

Most of you will already have your collection of power phrases, but there may be one or two here that you have not come across:
- Everyone should be given the chance to die just once without life insurance, and be able to look back at the problems they have left behind for others.
- There are two times that a person should not speculate: when they cannot afford it and when they can afford it.
- Life insurance should be bought as well as—not instead of—other investments.
- It is better to have something you may not need than to need something you cannot have.
- There are too many rich widows and not enough rich widowers.
- The only difference between a wife/husband and a widow/widower is the death of her husband/his wife.
- Anyone who is having trouble arranging financing at the bank should give more consideration to owning a large life insurance policy in order that they can become their own banker in the future.
- Beware of half truths—the half you get may be the wrong half.
- Life insurance policies do not have to be paid from income. They can be paid from transfer of assets.

Other Points to Consider

- God gives us each a head and a tail. Which one you use is yours to choose, but remember heads you win, tails you lose.
- God thought so much of you that He only made one of you.
- You are the best you that you know, so make the most use of the only you that you know.
- People would rather know how much you care than care how much you know.
- A short pencil is better than a long memory.

- Being well dressed and speaking grammatically correct will not make a sale for you, but it will not lose you one either.
- When a client asks how much any specific life insurance policy will cost, ask that client when he or she is going to die, then you can tell them how much it will cost. (This may seem like a cheeky answer, but, in fact, no one really knows how much any life insurance policy will cost.)
- Be a giver, not a taker. It becomes known.
- More time on preparation saves time on presentation.
- A bad reputation precedes you much faster than a good one.
- It is better to be over the hill than under it.
- If people knew how long they were going live, they would take better care of themselves while they were young.
- A 747 is quite an airplane. It can carry 450 people across the Atlantic in a few hours, but have you ever seen it float? No? That is because it is not designed to float. Permanent life insurance is similar. It will not do everything, but the things that it is designed to do, it does well!

All through your career you will come across many statements that may sound strange but it is amazing how a little story can paint a picture.

FIFTEEN

Life Insurance and the Banker

This chapter has been written specifically for bankers, but anyone may find the information useful when dealing with bankers. I will be discussing:

- marketing;
- present lending practices;
- running a family as a small business; and
- general financing.

Marketing

Just as the insurance industry has changed over the years, so too has banking. Marketing has become a major factor in both businesses. I would like to see more co-operation between bankers and insurance agents.

I have been in the life insurance business for over fifty years, and I am sure that I do not need to tell you just how hard life insurance is to market. The business is so negative that as soon as many agents can live within their income they will not try to sell any more, simply because they cannot take the constant negativity associated with the product.

I have found over the years that people are not really adverse to life insurance—only the fact that they have to pay for it. In one's early days of income earning there are always places for one's dollars that seem to take priority over life insurance. However, when I ask if money was no object, would they buy life insurance, the answer is usually yes.

It would appear that it is not life insurance that is the problem—it is paying for it. This is where co-operation between banker and insurance agent comes in.

People should make more use of the various services banks have to offer. For instance, I recommend that my younger clients take out personal loans in order to purchase adequate life insurance to protect their family. The majority of people are actually better off than they think they are. Unfortunately, they do not understand how to make the most of their present assets and future potential income.

I am constantly amazed by the way in which some bankers at the local level can be of so much assistance to clients, while others appear to be unwilling to help at all. Because of this lack of consistency at the local level I would like to direct my comments to the boards of directors and the marketing departments of the major banks in the hope that some guidelines may be established from the top, rather than attempt to convince individual branch managers of the benefits of my suggestions. Although bankers are not supposed to moralize, unfortunately some do.

Present Lending Practices

I feel that there have been inequities in lending principles, particularly at the consumer-loans level. Most consumer and personal loans are granted on a net debt ratio or gross debt ratio basis, and small business loans are granted on a working capital ratio basis (ratio of liquid assets to current liabilities).

I would prefer to see banks consider working capital ratio for some consumer loans, as it is a recognized fact that people will make sacrifices in order to obtain items that they wish to have and could have if consumer loans were handled on a working capital ratio basis. It seems to be rather a high-handed attitude for a banker to tell a customer just how much they can or cannot afford to pay from their income in a month.

Banks should also consider consumer loans on a working capital ratio basis as they do with businesses. My reasoning here is that if any business had a two-times working-capital ratio, then the loan would be considered excellent. If that business had only a one-times working-capital ratio, it would still be considered to be a good loan. But, in actual fact, many business loans are granted with less than one-times working-capital ratio. Several are run constantly on a working-capital deficiency. These businesses require a monthly cash flow from operations to service their loan. By using the method of cash-flow financing that I suggest, some consumer loans already have between two- and three-times working-capital ratio, making the loans very secure; yet some of these loans may not qualify under the debt-ratio requirements.

It is for that reason that there are more bad loans granted to businesses than to consumers. Business loans do not qualify under debt-ratio requirements.

A customer could easily qualify on a working-capital-ratio basis, but have difficulty qualifying on a net-debt-ratio basis.

I see nothing wrong in using liquidity to make loan payments in the event of a temporary setback, rather than surrendering the liquidity and applying it to the loan in order to reduce the monthly payment. In many cases the reduced payment does not help the situation. Sometimes a temporary setback creates the same problem for a small payment, but with a two- to three-times working capital ratio that customer would have two- to three-year loan payments covered by liquidity. If the customer ended up with only half of the original liquidity at the end of the loan the bank would still have done that customer a service.

Banks should now be considering a closer affiliation with the insurance companies. Insurance companies are moving toward providing a full range of financial services and could easily end up competing with the banks for their share of the money market.

There are already submissions to the government requesting the updating of insurance legislations in order to allow insurance companies to provide consumer loans for the purchasing of life insurance and annuities, and to market government securities, including Canada Savings Bonds, and many other proposals with which to extend the powers of life insurance companies. Instead of having allies, the banks could find that they have serious competition.

Running a Family like a Small Business

As bankers you are aware of the following facts and principles: A good rule for running a small business is to try to keep a strong working-capital position. The working-capital ratio is the ratio of current assets to current liabilities. Current assets are assets that are in the form of cash or can be converted into cash in the near future, usually twelve months (listed in order of liquidity). Current liabilities are liabilities due immediately or within the next twelve months.

current assets − current liabilities = working-capital ratio

A good rule is to have one's working capital more than twice one's current liabilities. This is hard to accomplish for most small businesses, but it is possible for many families. For example, if a couple were to borrow $25,000 at 15 per cent over five years, the approximate monthly payment would be $600. Therefore the current liability would be $7,200 per year, and the couple could use the money in the following manner:

$25,000
(5,000) RRSP
$20,000 Balance
(4,000) New premium – first-year cash value more than $2,000
$16,000 Balance
(3,000) leave in daily account for emergency
$13,000 Balance
(13,000) term deposits
$0 Balance

Liability	Security		
$25, 000 or	$13,000	term deposits	} Cash security
	$3,000	cash	
$600 per month	$5,000		} Semi-liquid security
until paid	$2,000	first-year cash value	
(current liability	$2,000	tax savings at 40%	} Cash within 12 months
$600 x 12 = $7,200)	$1,920	interest at 12%	
	$26,920		

Working-capital ratio based on cash security
(term deposits + daily account):
$16,000 ÷ $7,200 = 2.2 ratio

Working-capital ratio based on including RRSP funds:
$21,000 ÷ $7,200 = 2.7 ratio

Working-capital ratio based on total security within twelve months:
$26,920 ÷ $7,200 = 3.7 ratio

None of these calculations take into account any cash flow from income that may be available in excess of the $600 payment.

$$\frac{\text{Liquidity} + \text{Net income}}{\text{Total current liability}} = ?$$

Loan
Mortgage
Food
Gas
Telephone
Utilities
Pocket
Balance of cash flow

General Financing

If bankers took a bit more time with their clients, they could show many of them how to arrange their finances to allow them to accomplish some of the following:

- Borrow for investment purposes.
- Take advantage of the privilege clauses in their mortgage.
- Purchase a new car within a five-year repayment schedule instead of a used car over three for the same monthly outlay.
- Purchase adequate coverage on a permanent basis while they are young and healthy, rather than purchase term insurance and convert it piece by piece as they grow older.

They would be doing a great service to their customers.

SIXTEEN
Life Insurance and the Politician

This may be a fruitless exercise, but hopefully my message may get through to those politicians who recognize that, as an elected representative, they have an obligation to the voters. The areas I'll address are new legislation and social recognition.

New Legislation

Over the past few years various governments have legislated changes in life insurance. Some proposals have been implemented while others have been withdrawn, thanks mainly to the efforts of the Life Underwriters Association of Canada on behalf of Canadians.

It is amazing that any government would want to make purchasing life insurance any more complicated to people than it already appears to be. Perhaps the government doesn't realize that life insurance and the family home are the two major items that make up the average Canadian's estate. (On reflection, perhaps they are aware of the fact, and view these areas as unimportant.) In what other country in the world has a government attempted to tax the death benefit of life insurance? Life insurance is one of the few ways left to the average Canadian to protect family in the event of early death, or to ensure a comfortable retirement for themselves. Each step the government takes to make this more difficult is nothing short of irresponsible.

I would like to see the government provide more assistance in the areas of life insurance and personal residences. I would like to see a special low mortgage rate that would remain constant for the duration of a mortgage, rather than the present fluctuating rates which, when combined with the one-, three-, and five-year mortgages, can penalize homeowners by as much as 5 per cent if their mortgage happens to be open at the wrong time. How can anyone plan for a 5 per cent swing in interest rates? Many families have lost their homes, or have run into very hard times, because of this fact alone.

I would also like to see the government legislate a tax deduction for at least a portion of permanent insurance premiums for any Canadian who has enough interest in providing for the future—be it for the policyholder or her family.

Social Recognition

The social recognition of life insurance is based on the idea that any Canadian wishing to help provide for his retirement, or the well-being of his family in the event of his death, should be encouraged to do so. Life insurance is a vital part of personal security.

Life insurance companies are a major source of mortgage money for many Canadians.

I believe that countries such as the United Kingdom, Australia, Germany, and South Africa have recognized the importance of life insurance, and allow deductions from taxable income for life insurance premiums.

For some low-income families, life insurance is the only form of estate held. This allows a certain amount of reassurance and saves the public purse. Surely politicians recognize that any steps that discourage the protection of dependants through life insurance may result in increased costs in social assistance.

One final point: In this age of high unemployment, government assistance with mortgages as well as the allowance of greater contributions to RRSPs would result in more people having the opportunity of taking early retirement; this in turn would make more room for young people entering the work force.

SEVENTEEN
Life Insurance and Businesspeople

This chapter will illustrate the advantages of corporate-held life insurance.

In Ontario small businesses have a tax break of 16.5 per cent as long as the company earns an annual income of $400,000 or less. Once they go above this amount they are subject to the standard tax rates of 45 to 50 per cent. Investment income does not generally qualify for the small business deduction and possibly be taxed at the higher corporate tax rates. Excess of funds in your business that are not required for operations they are generally left in the business and invested in passive income-earning investments, or simply withdrawn for personal use.

When these excess funds are passed to an individual, they are taxed again at the personal tax rate for the income or dividends received, yet the corporation may claim a refund from the refundable dividend tax on hand (RDTOH) account to help prevent double taxation.

Let's look at an example. A holding company is set up to receive any excess funds for traditional investments.

Capital in taxable investment:
1. Tax on personal income, assume 46 per cent rate.
2. Tax on the investment growth, assume 50 per cent.
3. The refundable dividend tax on hand (RDTOH) account helps prevent double taxation of the investment income earned.
4. The private corporation pays additional tax when it earns investment income. It can recover this additional tax at a rate of one-third of the taxable dividends paid to shareholders.

Corporate-held Life Insurance at Death

The holding company is the owner of the policy. The operating company is the beneficiary of the policy. The premiums are paid by way of inter-corporate dividends (at the 16.5 per cent tax rate) to the holding company for the policy.

When the death benefit is paid to the corporation the proceeds in excess of the adjusted cost base are credited to the capital dividend account (CDA). The corporation can then pay the tax-free capital dividends of the CDA to the surviving shareholders or estate.

The advantage of corporate-held life insurance allows a business to preserve more of its assets for transfer to heirs and allow the surviving shareholders to make fair decisions without dissolving the company. Basically, you have the ability to pay tax-free dividends to the surviving shareholders.

Corporate-held Life Insurance While Living

The corporation can reduce the tax it pays each year on the growth of fixed-income investments by using some or all of its passive assets to pay premiums for a permanent life insurance policy.

The tax-advantage growth will increase funds to be used for other business and investment opportunities. It can also used to pay out additional expenses and deal with unforeseen emergencies such as downturns in the markets, slower operating growth, and so on.

Here are ways to access the cash values in the policies:

- Collateral loan: a series of loans against the security of the cash value from a bank, at the current prime rate (no tax).
- Partial surrender: accessing the cash directly from the policy, i.e. dividend growth.
- Policy loan: borrowing directly from the policy, but a higher rate may be used.
- Secured line of credit: having the policy held as security, to have a secured line of credit at prime interest only, and pay on what's being used. This is always the best option, because you have an ever-increasing line of credit at prime (no tax).

When operating companies are growing, a holding company is a great place to move assets to contain your excess earnings, and a life insurance policy will allow you to keep operations ongoing from a tax-preferred basis by way of permanent life insurance.

EIGHTEEN
Life Insurance and the Professional

Professionals have different problems. It is an accepted fact that if you spend more years and money to become a professional in your chosen vocation you will usually earn better than average income to justify the investment of time and money.

Young professionals quite often graduate with sizeable student loans and if they go into private practice there is the added cost of setting up a practice—renting office space, equipment, and staff—before they are even established. Fortunately, their earnings are higher to offset these costs and the banks will in most cases lend money to professionals for the above expenses based on their future potential income.

But everything depends on the professional. If she died or became disabled there would be no practice, which means greater needs for insurance, and not only life insurance. Professionals have to consider disability insurance, critical illness insurance, business interruption insurance, and liability insurance.

Most professional associations provide large amounts of term insurance and it is comparatively inexpensive when the professional is young—but the premiums can become prohibitive in later years. I suggest that professionals consider purchasing permanent life insurance when they are young. The premiums never change, the coverage increases to fight inflation, and the cash value can be used as an operating account for the practice, creating some tax-free savings, and eventually supplementing early retirement.

There is nothing wrong with putting the maximum amount into RRSPs if there is money available and putting the tax savings back into the operating account.

Professionals are also responsible for their own retirement and are advised to make maximum contributions to RRSPs. Young professionals making the maximum RRSP contributions from starting practice until retirement amass a large sum for retirement. Thirty years ago it was unusual to find anyone with $50,000 to $100,000 in an RRSP. Today it is not unusual to find people with $500,000, $1,000,000 or $2,000,000 in RRSPs, and they are all grumbling about the tax they have to pay.

Some major accounting firms advocate purchasing permanent life insurance on the parents to pay the tax on the parent's unused portion of RRSPs or potential capital gains, instead of purchasing RRSP's on themselves.

In the past, financial advisers recommended buying term insurance and investing the difference in an RRSP. The problem with term insurance is that most term insurance plans terminate at sixty-five. Ten-year terms terminate at age seventy-five, and fifteen-year terms at eighty.

There is Term to 100 (Universal Life) with a side fund that can be invested in the market and it qualifies as a permanent policy; however, the premium for Term to 100 can be prohibitive and because the side fund is invested in the market, the bank will advance only 50 per cent of the side fund to use as your operating account as opposed to 100 per cent in a permanent life insurance policy. Remember that with term insurance, the longer you live, the larger portion you pay of your own death benefit as the face amount remains the same.

At one time London Life was purely a life insurance company until we became a total financial planning company at the cost of our life insurance business. I am happy to see a swing back toward permanent life insurance as I am totally biased toward the purchase of permanent life insurance and the 20-Pay-Life policy in particular.

NINETEEN
Actual Presentation Used over the Years

Section 1: Life Insurance and the Single Person

Single people can sometimes be the hardest to convince that life insurance is a good deal, and the younger they are the better the deal. Some of them tell me they don't need life insurance and I have to agree, statistically they don't need life insurance, they should live enough to get married, raise a family, purchase a house, enjoy some luxuries in life, save enough to retire comfortably, and leave a reasonable estate to their children.

When I ask them about life insurance they tell me they are not married, they don't have a mortgage, nobody depends on them and they already have a policy that their parents bought for them when they were born. (Strike One)

When I ask them about RRSPs, they tell me they just started work and they have plenty of time to think about retirement. (Strike Two)

What about investments? They tell me, Bob, the best investments when you are young are wine, women, and song (WWS) and frankly I do agree with them; and when I suggest that they spend $500 per month on WWS, some of them tell me $1,000 and more a month. In fact, the only amount they save is $200 per month so that they can have their WWS in Barbados once a year. (Strike Three)

Let's look at the people spending $500 per month, or $6,000 per year, on entertainment, and ask if they might consider making their money do more than one job on the premise that while people work eight hours a day, money works twenty-four hours a day. That same monthly $500 could do a lot without forfeiting their lifestyle.

If you qualified at the bank for a $25,000 unsecured line of credit at 2 per cent repay, and you were using the total $25,000, your payment would be $500; even if the interest was 10 per cent ($25,000 × 10% = $2,500 / 12 = $208 interest) and $292 principle as savings; and they would have the use of $25,000.

The first step is to put $6,000 into a thirty-day term deposit and renew it each month for $5,500, $5,000, $4,500, etc. so that you do not do without your entertainment. You would still have $19,000 available to purchase a one-time deposit to an RRSP of $5,000, which saves you some tax—you still have $14,000 available to purchase $4,000 premium (first-year cash value of approximately $2,000) and $10,000 in a GIC. (Nowadays I would probably suggest a $10,000 premium, with a first-year cash value of approximately $5,000 and put $4,000 into GICs for emergencies.)

If you run your total income through this line of credit, using your line of credit as your operating account, you will find that there is sufficient principal paid down to take care of next year's premium, next year's RRSP, and the trip to Barbados.

If you paid $850 per month to the bank for the past twelve months it indicates you could have borrowed a larger amount of money:

$42,000 at 7% over 5 years = $837 monthly

$42,000
 16,550 previous balance of first $25,000 loan
$25,450
  4,000 second-year premium—policy worth $5,000
$21,450
  5,000 second-year RRSP saves another $1,500 tax
$16,450
  6,000 entertainment
$10,450 to do with as you will

Section 2: Using Life Insurance to Purchase a Car

There are many different investment philosophies; some people invest in their own business or real estate, some in Canada Savings Bonds, mutual funds, or the stock market; but very few people consider permanent life insurance as an investment vehicle.

What do you feel is a fair interest return on an investment today? Is that figure before or after tax? Would you agree that an investment is only an estate value if you do not or cannot use it? (A person's estate value is his or her net worth on the day that they die.)

Decide what interest you think you can earn and what tax bracket you expect to be in during the accumulation years. You'll find you cannot earn a high interest rate and remain in a low tax bracket. As your earned income increases due to either inflation or profitability, and your investment income increases from accumulation, you enter a higher tax bracket, which lowers your net interest income after tax. As you can see, investments can create their own monster: the more you make, the less you get to keep after taxes!

I want to compete with the values in your operating account, not with investment values. What do you earn on your operating account? Is that figure before or after tax? You can effectively earn compound interest on your operating account if you use your policies as your future operating account. Remember, I do not just sell life insurance policies, I sell future operating accounts. Let's compare the estate and cash values of an investment with those of a permanent life insurance policy (i.e. operating account). If you invested $10,000 annually for any given number of years to age forty-five at 3 per cent compound interest after tax versus investing the same amount each year into a $428,473 20-Pay-Life policy:

	Estate Value ($)		Cash Value ($)	
Years	Investment	Policy	Investment	Policy
5	54,680	577,382	54,680	42,167
10	118,808	738,492	118,808	106,106
15	191,570	896,084	191,570	192,896
20	276,760	1,098,698	276,760	310,537
30	371,965	1,498,881	371,965	568,626

There is no doubt which is the best estate value at all times, and even the cash value of the policy competes with the investment in the later years. But you have to remember that the investment figures are based on compounding interest, which means you cannot use these funds, even temporarily, without upsetting the compound factors!

Whereas you can borrow 100 per cent of the cash value of a policy at a favourable interest rate, on your own repayment terms, and pay it back into your own tax-free savings account as many times as you wish during the accumulation years without upsetting the final figures, which makes a policy a perfect operating account.

Think about this: since most people change their cars every two to five years, a half-decent car will cost about $80,000 ten years from now. Usually people either use their savings or investments or borrow from the bank. A permanent life insurance policy gives you a third choice. Let's take a look at each option:

1. Using money from an investment

Assuming you invested $10,000 each year for the next ten years at 3 per cent compound interest after tax, which is a realistic figure today:

Value of investment—tenth year $118,808
Less purchase price of car   80,000
Left to earn compound interest $ 38,808

Each time you borrow from savings or an investment, you forfeit the compound interest on that money forever!

2. Borrow from the bank

Some people seem to have difficulty understanding life insurance, but they all understand the following:

Purchase: $80,000 car loan from bank.
Payments over 5 years = $1,547.20 × 60 months = $92,832
You pay $12,832 interest on $80,000 at 6% average prime.
You cannot miss a payment.
You don't own the car until the loan is paid.
Every payment you make to the car is going into the bank, not into your account.
The car is worth half of what you have paid at the end of the five years! When the car is paid you have no cash available so you have to borrow again for your next car or purchase. Your available cash is nil! If you borrow from the bank, you pay the interest and principal back to the bank at their repayment terms.

3. Use money from policy

Translate annual premium $10,000 ÷ 12 = $833.33 per month
Use $80,000 from policy tenth year.
Stop paying premium (as such).
Just repay car payment to policy instead of the bank

$833 to premium increases policy
714 to loan × 60 months
$1,547

$192,896
− 106,106 = $ 86,790
= 42,840

Approximate Cash = $129,630
Plus $26,106 not previously used + 26,106
$155,736

Plus balance of cash flow
Plus insurance coverage paid

This method allows you to pay the interest and principal back into your own tax-free savings account at your own repayment terms to suit your budget.

Pay Cash for Car: Car Payment Back to Investment

VALUE OF INVESTMENT FROM TENTH TO FIFTEENTH YEARS
$38,808 × 5 years × 3% compound interest = $ 44,978
$1,547 × 12 = $18,564
× 5 years × 3% compound interest = $101,508
$146,486

VALUE OF POLICY IN FIFTEENTH YEAR

	Estate Value	Cash Value
	$896,084	$192,896
Less Balance of Loan	37,160	37,160
Net Estate Value	$858,924	$155,736

Original Loan	$80,000
Repaid	42,840
Balance	$37,160

As you can see, borrowing from your policies does cost you interest. You don't get anything for nothing: money does cost money. However, the major difference between borrowing from the bank and using your policies as your operating account is that when you borrow from a bank you repay the interest and principal back to the bank at their repayment terms, and you can reborrow only the principal. Whereas, if you use your policies as your operating account, when you repay the interest and principal back into your own tax-free savings account, at your own repayment terms, you can reborrow both the interest and the principal.

Doesn't that make more sense? If any of these loans are not repaid at the time of a claim, the insurance company will deduct the interest and principal outstanding with a minimal effect on your estate value.

It's fair to assume that if you were to purchase your future cars, vacations, etc., from the bank that these loans will be paid off before retirement. Then is it also fair to assume that if you borrow from your policy to buy these items, these loans would also be paid off before retirement? Therefore, all the money would be back in your policies to supplement early retirement.

Section 3: Using Life Insurance to Purchase a House

Bankers are in the business of lending money, but they want to know what you are going to do with the money and how you intend to repay the money you borrowed. Many people purchase their first house with a 5 to 10 per cent down payment just to get into the market and save paying rent.

This presentation can give you some ideas about the various options you have with the same amount of money available each month. I have helped many people purchase houses with a line of credit as opposed to a mortgage.

Purchasing a House (Using $100,000 or 100 per cent of the Purchase Price)

If you purchase a house with as little as 5 or 10 per cent down payment, you would have what is called a high-ratio mortgage.

With a high-ratio mortgage, there is an Mortgage Insurance Company of Canada (MICC) or Central Mortgage Housing Corporation (CMHC) charge of approximately $3,500 with a 5 per cent down payment or $2,500 with 10 per cent down. This charge is added to your mortgage, which means you pay interest and principal on this amount on top of the mortgage.

You could have a traditional mortgage with a 25 per cent down payment amortized over twenty-five years with certain privilege clauses. Or you could use a line of credit 25 per cent down payment at prime with payments on the principal to suit your budget.

Here are some methods to save a down payment of 5, 10, or 25 per cent in one year:

- $5,500 ÷ 12 = $458.00 per month plus some interest.
- $10,500 in one year ÷ 12 = $875.00 per month plus some interest.
- $25,500 in one year ÷ 12 = $2,125.00 per month plus some interest.

Assume only $458.00 per month is available, $875 per month is possible, and $2,125 per month is highly unlikely.

Assuming only $458 per month is available for payments: with the proper presentation you could request a loan of $75,000 to purchase thirty-day term deposits or GICs.

$75,000 × 6% average prime interest = $4,500 ÷ 12 = $375

- The loan is fully secured.
- The term deposits or GICs earn some interest.
- Every dollar in excess of the interest is saving you 6 per cent after tax.
- The interest charges on money borrowed to earn interest are tax deductible.
- If you apply the difference between the interest payment and the $458 available on the loan; if you apply the interest earned on the GICs to the loan and if you apply the tax saving on the loan, you are only trading dollars.
- You could be marginally ahead depending upon how much you earn on the certificates and your tax bracket.
- This should be a no-brainer for the bank, but it won't do a lot for you.

Did you know that you can borrow different amounts for the same money each month depending on the security and the length of payment? Here's an example using 8 per cent and $458 per month:

$14,000 over 3 years = $438
$22,000 over 5 years = $446
$37,000 over 10 years = $448
$68,000 interest only = $453

All the above payments are less than $458 per month.

	$14,000	$22,000	$37,000
Purchase $10,000 premium	10,000	10,000	10,000
First-year cash value approx	$4,800		

(same as saving $400/month for next 12 months)

	$ 4,000	$12,000	$27,000
RRSP	4,000	5,000	10,000
	0	$ 7,000	$17,000
GIC	7,000	17,000	
	0	0	

With the proper presentation you could request:

$75,000 × 6% = $4,500 ÷ 12 = $375 interest only per month

$75,000
−10,000 New premium first-year cash value $5,000 ÷ 12 = $458
$65,000
−15,000 RRSP saves approximately $5,250 (35%) tax ÷ 12 = $437
$50,000
−50,000 GIC × 6% = $3,000 ÷ 12 = $250 per month

Security		Potential Payment
$50,000	GIC	$ 458 Savings (Available)
+ 5,500	Policy	+ 437 Tax Rebate
+15,000	RRSP	+ 250 GIC interest
$70,500		$1,145 (on loan)

− 375 Interest at 6% average
$ 770 (principal) × 12 = $9240

		New Security	
$75,000	Original loan	$35,000	GIC
− 9,240	Less principal	+ 4,000	Policy
$65,760		+21,900	RRSP
		$70,900	

$10,000 Next-year Premium
+ 5,000 RRSP
$15,000

Let's say the reason there is only $458 available for payment is that you are paying $800 per month in rent. (Compare payments before loan with payments after loan.) If you can arrange to get everything you owe to the lowest rate possible, you can't do any better, which is one of the objectives.

With the proper presentation you could request the same $75,000 part secured, part unsecured (new rules 2 per cent repay).

$75,000
<u>–25,000</u> down payment (creating $25,000 equity in house)
$50,000
<u>–10,000</u> new premium (The second-year premium is available at interest only at prime)
$40,000
<u>–10,000</u> one-time deposit to RRSP
$30,000
<u>–30,000</u> GICs
    0

- The down payment exchanges rent of $800 to interest only of $375 on $75,000.
- The new insurance of $200,000 on each spouse allows either of them to purchase the house in the event of a premature death.
- The first-year cash value of the $10,000 premium is approximately $4,800, which is the same as saving $400 per month for the next twelve months—the first step to your future operating account.
- The $10,000 RRSP saves approximately $3,000 tax / 12 = $250 per month (which you wouldn't get if you didn't borrow the money).
- The $30,000 GIC for emergencies, to earn some interest and make a part of the loan tax deductible (interest on money borrowed to earn income is tax deductible).

Payments before request:	rent	$ 800
	savings available	<u>458</u>
		$1,258

Payments after request:

	Payment	Interest
$25,000 house, interest only on $75,000	$375	$375
30,000 GIC Security ($30,000 × 6% = $1,800 ÷ 12 = $150)	150	150
<u>20,000</u> Unsecured at 2% repay	<u>400</u>	<u>100</u>
$75,000	$925	$625

Every dollar in excess of the interest becomes principal or savings. All you have to do is trust the math. The bank should consider this a good loan because it has a new customer who has used many of the bank's services: loans, RRSPs, GICs, and credit cards. In addition, you have purchased life insurance to protect everything and start your future operating account.

Section 4: Freedom 55 is Not Just an Advertising Slogan

Pre-Retirement Planning

Whether you think you need them or not, set up maximum lines of credit on your house, policies and non-registered investments. The reason for this is that qualification is necessary: If you qualify for maximum lines of credit based on net-debt and gross-debt ratios while you are working, they will not be taken away when you retire.

Points to Consider

- London Life is part of the Great-West Life organization that includes Investor's Group and Canada Life, so we are in an even better position to do complete financial planning.
- We have access to all of the mutual and segregated funds, and have the ability to broker all products. I have chosen to specialize in permanent insurance as I believe it covers the most important aspect in financial planning.

The four major areas to be considered in a financial plan are:
- liquidity (80 per cent of house and 90 per cent of cash value)
- family security (five to ten years income)
- retirement (RRSPs); and
- disability (group or personal).

Our objective is to get your total indebtedness to interest only at prime, payments on the principal to suit you, as soon as possible.

There are only two places you can accumulate liquid capital at prime without attracting tax: 80 per cent of the value of your principal residence and at least 90 per cent of the net cash value of your policies. All other forms of investment earn an interest income which is taxable, dividend income which is taxable, capital gains which are taxable, and RRSPs, which are taxable when withdrawn. You pay enough tax on income and you do not want to pay tax on your savings and investments.

151

You'll find that life insurance can be better than RRSPs at retirement, although it can be hard argument to win.

Formula for "Freedom 55"

Invest 25 per cent of your gross income into life insurance premiums and you'll find it will provide adequate coverage, and collateral for your operating account, and eventually supplement early retirement.

Basic Rule of Thumb

Income	25%
$ 40,000	$10,000
$ 60,000	$15,000
$ 80,000	$20,000
$100,000	$25,000

A quarter of your gross income is hard to do in the early years without a bank's assistance, but it doesn't take many years until you become your own banker.

IDEAL SITUATION

Twenty-five-year-old earning $40,000 paying 25 per cent of gross for premium

Total premium $10,000 × 20 years = $200,000

VALUE OF POLICY AT AGE FIFTY-FIVE

Estate Value	Cash Value	Premium	Next Increase
$1,498,436	$568,626	Paid up	$33,105 After Tax

Points to Consider

USING 25 PER CENT OF $40,000 GROSS INCOME OR $10,000 PER YEAR $10,000 PURCHASES $428,473 – 20 PAY LIFE POLICY – AGE 25

1. Total premium $10,000 × 20 years = $200,000

VALUE OF POLICY IN ITS TWENTIETH YEAR (PRIMARY EXAMPLE)

Estate Value	Cash Value	Premium	Next Increase
$1,098,698	$310,537	Paid-up	$19,573

No More Premiums (Year 21)

2. The twenty-first-year increase is more than twice the premium ($19,573).

3. Increases in the first ten years after becoming paid up:

Value of Policy

	Estate Value	Cash Value	Premium	Next Increase
Age 55	$1,498,881	$568,626	Paid up 10 Years Ago	$35,179
Age 45	$1,098,698	$310,537		$19,573
Increase –	$400,183	$258,089		Increasing Each
No Payments				Year – No Tax

* More than the total of first twenty years' premiums. Note: Gross income at age twenty-five is $40,000. Net income at fifty-five is $33,105.

Even if there was a 25% reduction in dividends, are these figures so bad?

4. We now have to show a 25 per cent reduction in our dividends due to fluctuations in the market and use of universal life policies.

Value of Policy

	Estate Value	Cash Value	Premium	Next Increase
Age 55	$1,166,453	$453,390	Paid up 10 Years Ago	$25,003
Age 45	$905,558	$264,494	Paid Up	$14,745
Increase	$260,895	$188,896	Increasing Each Year – No Tax	
No Payments				

USING 25 PER CENT OF $40,000 GROSS INCOME OR $10,000 PER YEAR

1. Translate the $10,000 to $833 per month.

2. The $833 per month will satisfy a $40,000 loan over five years at 9 per cent interest from a bank to establish your credit while you are still young.

3. Analyze the loan:

$40,000

–10,000 RRSP that saves approximately

$30,000 $3,600 tax ÷ 12 = $300 per month

–10,000 premium is a first-year cash value approximately

$4,869 ÷ 12 = $406 per month

(at age twenty-five purchases $428,473 of 20 Pay Life).

$20,000

<u>−10,000</u> misc. small bill, credit card, etc.

approximately = $300 per month.

$10,000

<u>−10,000</u> GICs to earn some interest and make part of the loan
tax deductible

= <u>$50</u> per month.

0 $1,056 per month

Is there anything wrong with using the loan this way?
- The earlier you put money into an RRSP the longer it will compound (Rule of 72).
- Age and health are important factors in life insurance.
- Bank debt is lower than credit card debt.
- GICs are for emergencies or saving toward down payment on a house.

Life insurance and the personal residence end up being the best, if not the only, investment in the estate of the average Canadian; and neither was originally purchased as such, but rather as protection and shelter.

Most bankers would consider this a good loan because they have new customer who:
- has borrowed money;
- invested in a $10,000 RRSP;
- uses the bank's credit card;
- invested in GICs; and
- purchased life insurance for future protection and tax-free savings.

They are using five of the bank's services and if the banker is negative about the life insurance I do not refer clients to that bank.

STILL USING $40,000 GROSS INCOME
Net debt ratio 35 per cent, gross debt ratio 40 per cent

If you were to apply the gross debt ratio on the $40,000 loan
($1,333 per month, 40% of gross income):

1. 40% gross debt ratio ($16,000 ÷ 12) $1,333 per month
2. $10,000 RRSP tax rebate approx. $3,600 ÷ 12 $300 per month
   (which you wouldn't get if you didn't borrow)
3. $10,000 premium—
   first-year cash value $4,869 ÷ 12 = $406 ----
   (same as saving $462 per month for next 12 months)
4. $10,000 GIC earns interest to make a portion
   of the interest onthe loan tax deductible $50 per month

   sub-total **$1,683 per month**

   Less interest at 10%
   = $40,000 x 10% = $4,000 ÷ 12 −$333

   $1,350 principal
   × 12
   $16,200 principal
   +$4,869 cash value
   +$10,000 GICs
   toward down payment **$31,069**

Good bankers are worth a fortune so don't let them down. Remember, it is better to save by repaying than it is to save by saving. The more you repay the more you can reborrow, especially if you are borrowing for appreciating assets (i.e., life insurance, home, and RRSPs). You will never go wrong.

USING A $10,000 PREMIUM ILLUSTRATION REPRESENTING 25 PER CENT OF A $40,000 GROSS INCOME

The bank's criteria for lending is 35 per cent of your gross income as net-debt ratio and 40 per cent of gross income as gross-debt ratio. The other 60 per cent of your income is for food, gas, telephone, utilities, pocket money, and income tax. If you are under 40 per cent gross-debt ratio, your credit is considered to be safe. The ideal clients would be:

- a twenty-five-year-old earning $40,000 per year and still living at home;
- a young couple saving for a down payment on first house; or
- anyone who wishes to retire early.

TWENTY
Interesting Stories

My Two Best Clients

I met two of my best clients when they called to cash in policies of $25 per month, which they felt they could not afford, and could do better things with the money at that stage of their lives.

Needless to say, I was able to save the policies, showed them what they were giving up, and demonstrated the advantages of permanent life insurance during their lifetime. Today one of them is paying $10,000 premium per year for over $600,000 coverage and the other is paying $59,000 per year premium with over $5 million coverage. They have become real believers in the use of policies over the years.

Mary and Daphne

Mary, Florrie, and Daphne were nurses who rented in the same building as I did, and they worked at the St. Catharines General Hospital. In 1963, nurses earned only about $3,000 to $4,000 a year. Over the years they purchased policies from me.

Florrie married and moved to Kitchener. Mary and Daphne remained single, and moved to Montreal, purchased some more policies, then returned to St. Catharines. There they bought a house and purchased more insurance. The interesting thing about Mary and Daphne was that Daphne was the youngest of the three; that was, until the government introduced legislation stating that an employer could let you retire at fifty-five if you wanted. Guess what? Suddenly Daphne became fifty-five before Mary, and retired before her. They both enjoyed many years of retirement, and every time I visited them they always said "Thank the Lord for Bob Shiels" for making it possible for them to retire at fifty-five. Actually, they did it themselves. I only gave them advice.

The Fifty-Four-Year-Old Doctor

We had a fifty-four-year-old client who was a doctor. His wife left him the year before for a younger man, which was bad enough. He worked in his practice from January to March and earned $60,000. He was diagnosed with cancer in March, died in September of the same year, and his two sons had to do his final income tax return which included $60,000 from the practice and $270,000 in RRSPs. On the $330,000 income, the boys had to pay $153,000 tax.

But let me make the situation worse. What if the doctor had worked in his practice until November and had been killed in a car accident? His income would have been $300,000 from the practice and $270,000 from RRSPs. On the $570,000 the tax would have been over $250,000. That's a difference of over $100,000!

I am being facetious when I say be sure you die in January. Fortunately, he did have some personal life insurance to cover the tax, which meant his estate did get the RRSP proceeds.

The Seventy-Five-Year-Old Widow

I have written a case for $250,000 of permanent life insurance on a seventy-five-year-old widow, on the advice of her financial adviser, to cover her capital gains and tax on the balance of her RRIFs.

It is fortunate that she was still insurable or this vehicle would not have been available. The objective of the large life insurance policy is to transfer her taxable non-registered funds to the policy, where they are tax free, and have a place to put her pension, RRSP, or RRIF income, rather than increasing her taxable income.

TWENTY-ONE
Do You Want to be a Millionaire?

Not too long ago, $1,000,000 was considered a lot of money. Nowadays it is not strange to find that with the value of their house, RRSPs, pensions, and life insurance, the average Canadian's estate can be worth half a million to a million dollars.

I wish that when I was much younger that I could have known what I know now. I say this because I firmly believe that, with the proper guidelines at a relatively early time in your life, anyone can, without too much trouble, become a millionaire by the normal retirement age of sixty-five.

Take a moment to think back to when you were twenty-five, or even younger. If you had been asked to invest $3,130 each year (I have chosen that figure for a particular reason,) with the guarantee that you would be a millionaire by normal retirement age, I feel sure that you would have considered that an excellent idea. I am also sure that there are few of us who have not needlessly spent $3,130 every year since we were twenty-five years old. I'll show you how simple it can be.

You could go the straight accumulation route using the magic of compound interest. For example, if you invested $3,130 each year at various rates for the whole forty years from age twenty-five to sixty-five:

6%	$513,455
7%	$668,458
8%	$825,699
9%	$1,152,720
10%	$1,523,803

11%	$2,021,395
12%	$2,689,080

You will see from the table that if you earned between 8 and 9 per cent compound interest after tax for the whole forty years, you would be a millionaire by age sixty-five. But remember: These are compound interest figures, which means that you cannot use this money, even temporarily, without upsetting the compounding factor.

The basic problem with this method is that should you require emergency funds for whatever reason, it may prove difficult to set aside the $3,130 that you require each year in order to become a millionaire by sixty-five—assuming that you are able to earn between 8 and 9 per cent compound interest after tax consistently for the whole forty years. If you were to ask a bank manager today what he feels is a fair return on a fairly safe investment, he would probably tell you 5 to 6 per cent after tax.

As I've discussed, most young couples cannot afford to take advantage of compound interest for a long period of time. The above example requires an annual $3,130 investment for 40 years, totalling $125,200. On the other hand, if you invested that $125,000 in the form of $6,260 for twenty years to purchase a substantial ($250,000) 20 Pay Life permanent insurance policy, you provide immediate protection for your family. This is a safe, worry-free investment. You do not have the problem of tax reporting or short-term fluctuations in interest rates, and you will note from the table on page 160 that the estate value, which is the real investment value, is $2,479,923 at age sixty. However, you would be a millionaire at age sixty instead of sixty-five because, as you can see from the table, the cash value of the policy is $1,046,084.

The advantage of this method is that, should you require emergency funds for any reason, you have the flexibility of being able to borrow up to 90 per cent of the policy's cash value, or of temporarily not paying the premium, and be in a position of being able to put this money back in at your convenience as many times as you wish during the accumulation years without upsetting the final figures.

Compare the cash and the estate values of the investment method with the cash and estate values of the $250,000 Pay Life policy, using the same investment of $125,000:

Investment: $3,130 × 40 years = $125,200
Policy: $6,260 × 20 years = $125,200

Comparison of Investment and Policy

	INVESTMENT			POLICY		
	Total	Cash	Estate		Cash	Estate
	Payments	Value	Value	Premiums	Value	Value
Year	($)	($)	($)	($)	($)	($)
1	3,130	3,318	3,318	6,260	3,790	264,787
3	9,390	10,564	10,564	18,780	19,367	302,216
10	31,300	43,732	43,732	62,600	85,815	525,517
15	46,950	77,223	77,223	93,900	161,720	766,357
20	62,600	122,045	122,045	125,200	279,544	1,083,938
Age	Payments continue			Payments stop		
55	93,900	262,294	262,294		679,554	1,903,429
60	109,550	369,709	369,709		1,046,084	2,479,923
65	125,200	513,455	513,455		1,580,534	3,197,161

You can see which is the best estate value at all times, and even the cash value of the policy competes with the investment in the later years. The point to remember is that an investment is an estate value only if you do not or cannot use it.

Consider the picture at the end of the first year:

• If you invest $3,130 at 6 per cent compound interest for one year, you'll have $3,318 to spend.

Estate value $3,318 minus $3,318 = 0

If you invest $6,260 as an insurance policy premium (the first-year cash value $3,790), and you borrow 90 per cent of the cash value which is $3,411:

Estate value	$264,787
Less 90% cash value	3,411
	$261,376

Consider the figure again at the tenth year. Assume that ten years from now you need $25,000 toward a new car. Most people would use money from their savings and investments, or borrow from the bank. You would have three choices: use money from your investment, borrow from the bank, or use money from your policy.

If you use the money from your investment, and assuming that you had invested $3,130 each year at 6 per cent compound interest after tax for the past ten years, the value of your investment would be $43,732. After deducting the $25,000 for the car you would be left with only $18,732 with which to earn interest the following year. Each time that you use that money, even temporarily, you forfeit the compound interest on that money forever, not to mention the fact that the interest is all taxable as you replace the money in your investment.

If you borrow from the bank to avoid upsetting the compounding factor in your investment, you would (a) pay interest and principal back to the bank on its terms; (b) be unable to miss a payment; (c) not own the car until it is paid off; (d) know that every payment you made was going to the bank and not into your own account; and (e) know that when the time came to purchase your next car you would have no money in your account, so you would have to borrow from the bank again.

If you use the money from your policy, and I am going to suggest that you use $50,000 (double the $25,000) because you paid $6,260 instead of $3,130 for the past ten years, you would still have $85,815 – $50,000 = $35,815 available from your policy, and the estate value would be $525,517 – $50,000 = $475,517 (see the table on page 160).

The advantage of this method is that you pay the interest and principal back into your own account. As money does cost money, you still have to pay interest, but if you do not repay these loans then the insurance company simply deducts the interest and principal when you die. The big difference between a bank loan and a policy loan is that when you borrow from the bank you can reborrow only the principal, but if you have paid the interest and principal back to the policy then you can re-borrow both the interest and principal with minimal effect on your death benefit or estate value.

You will find that permanent life insurance can provide some peace of mind, along with a safe investment that can be used during your lifetime.

Now, my final illustration, which I am sure that most people will find hard to believe, and many advisers will consider impossible, but all that has to be done to confirm it simply check the past record of insurance companies:

Value of $6,260 invested for 40 years at various rates of compound interest after tax	Value of $6,260 invested in a policy for 20 years, based on present dividend scale
6%	$1,026,910
7%	1,337,108
Cash Value: $1,580,534	
8%	1,751,398
9%	2,305,256
10%	3,047,606
Estate Value: $3,197,161	
11%	4,042,790
12%	5,378,120

Even though you invested $6,260 for forty years, as opposed to paying premiums to the policy for only twenty years, the policy's cash value competes between 7 and 8 per cent. The estate value, which is the real investment value, competes between 10 and 11 per cent compound interest after tax in an account that you can borrow from at a favourable interest rate, and repay at your repayment terms as often as you wish during the accumulation years without upsetting the final figures. In other words, you can effectively earn compound interest in an operating account by using your policy or policies as your operating account.

I hope that by reading this book you will look at permanent life insurance from a fresh perspective. I have shown how it is possible for you to provide for your dependants, and at the same time maintain or achieve the lifestyle of your choice; and should you still happen to owe $200,000, $300,000, $400,000 or even $500,000 to your policy, because of investments in lifestyle, you would still leave an estate well in excess of $1,000,000.

To me lifestyle is the important word. You do not have to be a millionaire; you just have to be able to live like one. Always keep in mind that you don't have to die to win.

TWENTY-TWO
Case Histories

Everything up to this point has been theoretical. I've extolled the virtues of life insurance, and I am sure you have said, "That's all fine on paper, but does it work in practice?" Well, here are a few real-life examples as proof of the benefits of my recommendations.

Case #1: Bill and Doreen

Bill and Doreen are a retired couple around eighty years old. I have known them for as long as I have been in the life insurance business. They used to pay $11.37 per month for their total insurance. Today, they pay $266.06 per month.

They are typical of many families with whom I have dealt over the years. They started out with small policies, increased them, then bought some more on both themselves and their children. Over the years, they have used these policies to buy cars, vacations, and so on. In fact, I don't think Bill has ever bought a car that he didn't pay for with policies. (Every Friday night Bill would come into our office and tell my assisstants to put $300 on his car.)

Every time I recommended that they should increase their coverage, they felt that they would have trouble paying for that extra coverage, but somehow it all worked out the way in which I had suggested it would. So much so that they now have their house paid off, they have money in RRSPs, and they have no loans on their policies.

Many years back, I told them that this would happen, but it was hard for them to believe it at times. Now they have guided their children along these

163

same lines, and I am currently doing business with two of their children.

Case #2: Kevin and Debbie

Debbie is Bill and Doreen's daughter. She had a $25,000 policy that her parents had taken out for her in 1972. She joined the armed forces and in Nova Scotia met Kevin, who was also in the services. At that time Kevin owned a $25,000 policy that he had purchased through an agent in Trenton, Ontario.

In 1979 they came to Ontario to be married. As members of the armed forces their income was certainly within the range of being average. After I sat down with them, they purchased an additional $100,000 of whole life on Kevin and another $50,000 on Debbie.

Since then, using my system and advice, they have operated with bank loans. I reviewed their program with them, when they were home on leave, and they were extremely pleased with their financial situation. They had $13,000 in RRSPs, $6,800 cash value in their policies, plus $14,000 in the bank. They did not owe anyone at this point, and they were extremely grateful to me for getting them started on a good path. They have since taken out a $150,000 policy on each of their two sons.

I believe that this demonstrates the advantages of organizing a plan, and buying permanent insurance at an early age in order to achieve the lowest premium rates.

Case #3: Bill and Louise

Bill and Louise, like many other couples who came to Canada in the sixties, spent the first few years struggling to make ends meet while raising their family and paying a mortgage. They purchased a small policy for each of themselves and their children, and a term insurance rider to cover the mortgage. Now, their family is raised and gone, and their mortgage is paid off. They recently remortgaged their house for 75 per cent of the appraised value and with these funds they purchased their first new car, bought some new permanent insurance to cover the mortgage, maximized their RRSP contribution, put a down payment on some property in Florida, and put the balance into interest-earning investments in order to make a portion of the interest on their mortgage tax deductible. The total repayment is comparable with the amount of money that they are now able to save each month.

They find it easier to repay a loan than to save money. In this way, they can now enjoy a better lifestyle while they are repaying. All they have done is to change some of their thinking. There are a couple of different philosophies about real estate: Some people feel that they should have their mortgage paid off. Others, such as myself, and now Bill and Louise, feel that no one should have their mortgage paid off if there is an inflationary trend, or if there is anything we are doing without. We feel that you should remortgage and use the funds to purchase appreciating assets, especially if you haven't been contributing the maximum to an RRSP each year.

When you have equity in your house, and you are not maximizing your annual RRSP contribution, you are in effect retiring your house while you have to keep on working. By remortgaging, you pay off your mortgage, which is on a depreciating balance, with a deflating dollar. You will find that the money produced by the tax savings and accumulation in your RRSP will more than offset any cost of remortgaging, just as Bill and Louise are finding that they have improved their lifestyle today while providing for a more comfortable lifestyle in retirement.

Case #4: Billy and Robyne

In 1974, at the age of nineteen, Billy purchased $100,000 of permanent life insurance from me. He did this on the recommendation of his father who felt that my ideas were in line with his own. Billy's income at that time was approximately $6,000 per year. In 1978 when he married Robyne, his income was approximately $14,000 per year, which was an average salary. However, he purchased another $100,000 of life insurance on himself and $50,000 on Robyne.

I had an opportunity to review their entire program when they purchased a new home. I found that they had cash values of approximately $11,000 in their policies, RRSPs worth $10,000, term deposits of approximately $10,000, $3,000 in a savings account, and $5,000 worth of shares in the company where Bill is employed. In addition, they had $12,000 equity in a newly purchased home, plus another $25,000 equity in a condominium that they were selling. They also had a $17,000 bank loan, which would be paid off with the condo sale.

Needless to say, Bill and Robyne are extremely pleased with the concept that I discussed with them a few short years ago. They got off on the right track and they saved on a regular basis.

Many people find it easier to pay a bill than to save money, so why not let your bank loan be a bill? Of course your banker will not lend you the money in first place if your credit is not satisfactory, and you will find it easier to borrow if you are purchasing an asset with the borrowed money. Every case has its own particular merit.

Case #5: Mario

(Author's note: In this case history you will notice that Registered Home Ownership Plan [RHOSP] was used. Unfortunately, the government eliminated this tax shelter in 1985; however, I am leaving this case history in as I believe it is of great interest.)

In the early 1980s Mario stepped in out the rain one day to have a cup of coffee with his friend Steve, one of our young agents. At that time Mario was twenty-two, earning approximately $22,000, and had a $25,000 life insurance policy, plus group insurance at work. Steve's earnings were considerably less.

During the conversation Mario asked Steve how much life insurance he had. He was rather startled to learn the agent held $250,000 worth, and he started to ask Steve questions. As Steve was relatively new to the business he brought Mario in to see me, and I, in turn, started to ask questions of Mario.

"Is your car paid?"

"Yes."

"Do you have an RHOSP?"

"Yes, with two years' contributions."

"Excellent. Do you have any savings?"

"Yes."

"Do you mind telling me how much?"

"I have $18,000."

I asked him how he had accumulated $18,000 and he told me that he had worked part-time while he was at school, and had worked full-time for the past year and a half. He still lived at home where he didn't pay board; his parents preferred that he save to buy a house. As a result, Mario saved between $150 and $200 each week without sacrifice.

I rather threw him when I suggested that he borrow $25,000 from the bank. Borrowing was against his basic principles, and in any case, why should he borrow when he had $18,000 in the bank? My proposal was that he borrow $25,000 over a five-year period at approximately $680 per month. At that time the interest rate was about 21.25 per cent, but term deposits were paying 18 per cent; therefore, the differential was only 3.25 per cent. This is how it worked:

Amount of loan	$25,000
Present savings	18,000
	$43,000
Premiums for a $250,000 policy (he paid two years in order to date the policy back to age 21)	(6,000)
	$37,000
RHOSP (third-year contribution)	(1,000)
	$36,000
RRSP (maximum allowable)	(3,500)
	$32,500
Leave in daily account for emergencies	(4,500)
	$28,000
Term deposits	(28,000)
	$ 00

As the loan was for $25,000, and as Mario ended up with $28,000 in term deposits, the loan was considered to be for investment purposes and, as a result, the total interest charges were tax deductible. In essence, he used his own money to buy the assets and use the borrowed money to purchase the investments.

The following tables illustrate Mario's assets both before and after the loan:

Before the Loan

	Estate Net Worth ($)	Liquid Net Worth ($)
Savings	18,000	18,000
RHOSP	2,000	2,000
Life Insurance	25,000	0
Total	45,000	20,000

After the Loan

	Estate Net Worth ($)	Liquid Net Worth ($)
RHOSP	3,000	3,000
RRSP	3,500	3,500
Term Deposits	28,000	28,000
Daily Account	4,500	4,500
Life Insurance	275,000	0
Total	314,000	39,000

With the $680 payment, which was approximately what Mario had been saving, plus the interest and the tax rebate, he could potentially pay between $1,300 and $1,400 per month on his loan.

When Mario came in to see us one year later for his review I asked him how he had made out. He told me he had paid only $1,000 per month on his loan, and, thanks to the high interest rate, this had reduced his loan by only about $8,000. He had then borrowed that $8,000 back again and had put another $1,000 into his RHOSP, another $3,500 into his RRSP, and had paid the third year of his insurance premium.

I then asked him what he had done with the rest of the potential payment, and I was not surprised when he informed me that his term deposits were now up to $40,000.

By this time I felt I knew some of Mario's goals, so I asked him if he would rather have $40,000 in term deposits and a $250,000 policy that was three years old; or $37,000 in term deposits and a $250,000 policy which was three years old *plus* another $250,000 that would be one year old.

Mario thought about this for a minute, and he realized that premiums do not have to come from income, they can come from the transfer of capital. So, at age twenty-four, he purchased another $250,000 policy.

Here is an example of how some of Mario's assets looked at the end of the first year on this system:

After the First Year

	Estate Net Worth ($)		Liquid Net Worth ($)
RHOSP	5,000	plus interest	5,000
RRSP	7,500		7,500
Daily Account	3,000		3,000
Term Deposits	37,000		37,000
Life Insurance	525,000		4,000
Total	577,500		56,500

During the past year Mario has attended a couple of my seminars, and he asked a lot of questions.

Even with maximum contributions to his RRSP, Mario will still need a supplemental fund, which would be better accumulated in the form of cash values in a life insurance policy than in cash, which creates interest, which, in turn, creates taxable income.

When Mario was thirty-nine, his dividends alone were more than the annual premium. In that year his policy increased in cash value by $3 for every $1, and this fits very nicely into his plans for early retirement.

When Mario got married, he and his wife had no problem in buying the home of their choice. Let us assume that his wife had a take-home pay of $1,000 per month. Between them, they would be in a position to make a potential payment of $2,000 per month on a bank loan, and with that kind of debt service they will never have a mortgage on their house.

Yes, they will have a bank loan for a few years, but a bank loan is more flexible than a mortgage, and they will have only that loan until the cash value of their policies pay it off. At that time they will become their own banker with all the flexibility of policy loans.

It is a pleasure to do business with a young man like Mario. He doesn't think about the things that life insurance can't do for him. Instead, he is interested in the things that it can do to help him accomplish his goals.

Case #6: Doug and Annette

London Life has a university program for recruiting new agents, which gives graduates the opportunity to train at the company's head office. This is followed by a period out in the field, then back to head office, and finally, back to the field.

I had occasion to work with an agent who came to our local office through this program, and we worked together on several cases. He had some problems discussing life insurance with his friends so he invited me to work with him when he was talking to his best friends, Doug and Annette

While Doug was enthusiastic about my ideas, Annette was somewhat doubtful in the beginning. After considering and dissecting my proposals, she decided that there was a great deal of merit in what I was saying, and I consider her and Doug to be two of my greatest supporters. Since that time, they have held seminars at their home, inviting their parents and friends to hear my presentation, and they have also referred many people to me. I am truly grateful for their support.

We progressed in the same way we did when we first met: If Doug was absolutely enthusiastic about one of my suggestions, Annette went over it with a fine-tooth comb. She would ask a million questions then finally agree. It got to the point where it became a joke amongst the three of us, and Doug would say, "If Annette agrees, then it has to be good!" This was ideal to me. I want people to accept my recommendations because they make good sense, and not just because Bob Shiels was recommended to them by a friend.

When Doug and Annette had been on the program for only a few years, they had their house paid off, they each owned $250,000 of permanent life insurance, they had money in both term deposits and RRSPs, and they had a super track record at their bank where, yes, they do have a bank loan. They purchased $250,000 permanent life insurance on their infant son, and they purchased a new camper-truck in order to travel easier with their baby.

Their finances are in such good shape that Annette was able to stay at home with their baby. Finally, Doug applied for additional coverage of $250,000 on himself, which increased his coverage to over $500,000 with paid-up additions!

Do you wonder why I like my job? When I first met this wonderful couple they had all the hopes and ambitions one would expect: pay off their home, raise a family in comfort, enjoy a few luxuries. To see them achieve their goals and know that I had some small part in this gives me a great deal of satisfaction. The real credit, however, is theirs. All I did was to make some suggestions—they managed their money! They do not talk about Freedom 55—they talk about "Freedom 45."

Case #7: John and Gwen

This is a perfect example of a couple who do not need life insurance. Usually when I ask a couple if they have any miscellaneous assets such as a cottage up north, a condominium in Florida, land in Arizona, boats, Skidoos, coin collection, stamp collection, or anything else of consequence in their estate, their reply is no. However, when I asked these questions of John and Gwen, who are in their sixties, they had all of the above and more and, as a result, were going to leave a considerable estate to their family. They knew they were well off, but they did not feel that they had any extra money to spend.

They were quite excited, to say nothing of apprehensive, when I recommended that they remortgage their equity and purchase some new life insurance from transfer of assets, to replace the estate value for their children, and spend some of their liquid capital. They ended up purchasing new life insurance for themselves, for their children, and for their grandchildren. This way, instead of leaving their children cash in their estate, they would leave them with a ten-, fifteen-, or twenty-year-old policy on their lives, which the children cannot afford to buy for themselves at this stage; and the new life insurance on their own lives will allow the children to buy back the equity. They can leave their children a larger estate and have more to spend on themselves than if they continued trying to live on interest income.

Sometimes when I say a "young couple," it is relative to their life expectancy. John and Gwen are young in spirit and looking forward to twenty or perhaps thirty years of comfortable retirement.

Case #8: Marie and John

Marie and John are a nice young couple. Marie is the daughter of close friends of ours, and we had the opportunity of spending some good times with the couple at our friend's cottage up north. We would spend many hours talking about various subjects, ranging from the generation gap to their future aspirations. They were a joy to be with. Marie and John purchased their first life insurance policies from me shortly after graduating from university.

John's work as an engineer took them to Banff, Switzerland, Australia, upstate New York, and then on to Salt Lake City. Over the years they have become very good clients. They now have three children. Their first was born in Canada, the second in Switzerland, and the third in the United States, but all of their children's insurance, plus additional insurance on themselves, was bought through me.

With all the computer print-outs, long-distance telephones, and facsimile machines, it is almost as easy for me to service business overseas as it is for local business. To facilitate my out-of-town clients I have a private telephone number that only I answer, thus eliminating long-distance charges if I am out of the office when clients call.

"We met Bob shortly after coming to Canada. We did not know much about life insurance but we trusted him because we were also Scottish.

Over the years Bob guided us to purchase our first house then upgrade to our present house. We are now both retired. Our son and daughter are both married with children and, of course, have purchased life insurance from Bob.

It is a nice feeling, even though we are retired, to know that we have been able to purchase policies on our grandchildren, help both kids financially, still be able to go to Scotland every year, and have more than enough money than we need. We even bought a large policy at age sixty-nine to keep up with Bob's latest formula.

To let you know how much we listen to Bob's advice, I used to play squash in my forties, stopped playing, and he has me back playing squash with him five mornings a week at age seventy-seven. He has been a good friend over the years and we both agree that we would not be where we are without his help. He was the one who told us that you can't take your house to heaven with you, and there is nothing wrong with using the house to buy insurance; and the children and grandchildren can buy back the house with the insurance. Our son and daughter have bigger houses than us, but maybe one of the grandchildren may be interested."

—Bill and Louise McKenzie

"Looking back, we do remember telling Bob we couldn't afford the $11.37 per month premium and later telling him we could not afford $266 per month, but he was right. We now pay considerably more than that each year (more than $11,000).

Our house is paid off. We live very comfortably. We have money available we will never spend. In fact, there was a time when I invested $30,000 with Falloncrest and lost it. Bob tried to warn us but we told him it was money we weren't using anyway.

Bob hates to see money sitting not doing anything. He has been after us to put policies on our children or grandchildren."

—Bill and Doreen Smeed

"Our meeting with Bob Shiels over twenty-five years ago sent us on our way up the financial tree of life. Bob said you can climb the tree in many different ways, but you can't get halfway up, change your mind, come down again, try another way, get halfway up, change your mind, come down again. That way you will never get to the top.

Bob showed us a sure way to get to the top of the tree and told us that if it could hold his weight it could hold ours. It was a funny analogy at the time but it appealed to us and we stuck to his plan. As a result we built the house we always wanted, we travel, we drive the cars we want, we own a business, our daughter is in university getting her masters degree, and our son is an engineer. All the while our family was more than protected if anything were ever to happen to us.

Our next move is retirement and that too is taken care of. We bought life insurance to improve our lifestyle. Our hats go off to Bob Shiels. He would like to help you reach your dreams."

—Doug and Annette Thomson

"In the early 80s we phoned the local London Life office to cancel a policy that my husband had purchased many years before. The policy cost us $27.49 a month and at the time we were living paycheque to paycheque on one income with two small children. We lived in a house on which Don's mother held the mortgage, enabling us to afford it. I thought that we would be able to use the $329.88 that the policy cost us annually towards something more necessary. An agent met with us and suggested we meet Bob.

Needless to say, we did not cancel the policy.

Although the concept seemed to make sense when talking to Bob, it took us some time to fully understand what he was telling us. We started with a good deal of blind faith. Instead of cancelling a policy he had us buying more. Instead of paying off the house we were using its equity. Every time he came over for a revue of our position, Don just said, 'Ok

Bob, how much are you selling us this time?' And he showed us how in four years we were building a new home (kid number three made our home too small,) and within another five years we were in a position to purchase the business that my husband was working for. My kids, who are just becoming parents themselves, still refer to Bob as the 'Smarties man' because he always carried Smarties in his briefcase as a reminder of where he started.

Bob is now handling three generations of our family. My kids are in various stages with him, and buying policies on our new grandchildren just makes sense. We feel they don't need more toys, so for birthdays we pay for a 20-Pay-Life policy so when they turn twenty-one no premiums are required and they have their education paid for. What education fund can claim that? We have tried over the years to introduce other family members to this way of thinking, but some of them just don't get it. Those people are still wondering where their kid's education fund and/or retirement fund is going to come from.

Bob, we wish you good health for a very long time and are proud to consider you as part of our extended family."

—Don and Donna; Neal, Amy, Quinn and Baby #2;
and Michelle, Rob, Mady, and Rebecca

"Marie and I have known Bob and his lovely wife Anne since the early 1970s when we were just a young couple beginning our lives together. We spent many a visit with Bob discussing our lives, including our dreams of seeing the world, owning our own home, and having a family some day. Our lively conversations had a wide range of topics. Interestingly, both Marie and I never felt a generational difference during our visits with Bob and Anne, as we felt all our conversations were on the same level.

We bought our first policies when we were still in university at the age of twenty-one. After those first policies we continued to purchase more on ourselves and our children. Bob's advice of 'using our policies' made sense and helped us when we were starting out to get a good financial foundation. We still follow that advice.

My career allowed our family to travel and live all over the world. Yet with the vast amount of travelling, all our purchases and dealings with London Life and Bob were completely seamless. The whole life insurance also provided Marie and me the comfort of knowing that if anything happened to either of us the other would have a monetary safety net.

We must also say that Bob was very instrumental in coaching and helping us to become successful in our financial management and estate planning needs. Even though we are very conservative in our decisions regarding money and debt, his process helped us immensely as we applied it to our lives. Bob's approach to money management and life insurance go hand in hand, and is well worth a serious look to see how to apply it to your life."

—Marie and John

"I wish that I had met Bob Shiels a lot earlier in my life. I would have taken advantage years sooner of the life insurance, equity growth, and access to equity that Bob had introduced to me. I call this the 'triple effect' and I am convinced that I would be much better off today if I would have been able to take advantage of the extra years of investing with Bob. This in no way minimizes the benefit of following Bob's principles, regardless of age.

In my opinion the flexibility of the life insurance has given me the protection, investment growth, and cash availability that I will need to move forward into my later years."

—Ray Bretzloff

APPENDIX
Formula for Success Table

Highlight your age and apply my formula on page 181.

Age	Premium $10,000 Face Amount	1st year Cash Value	2nd Year Increase	Total	Cash Value 10th Year	Estate Value 20th Year	Cash Value 20th Year
0	$760,569	$5,174	$8,818	$13,992	$112,356	$2,590,913	$344,156
1	757,490	5,179	8,829	14,008	112,536	2,500,434	345,156
2	748,999	5,115	8,884	13,999	112,710	2,180,289	282,827
3	738,942	5,129	8,922	14,051	112,782	2,322,632	344,884
4	725,194	5,143	8,946	14,089	112,531	2,239,885	344,282
5	703,383	5,030	8,954	13,984	111,179	2,139,156	340,191
6	685,348	5,003	8,918	13,921	110,738	2,063,666	338,976
7	662,067	4,989	8,722	13,711	110,204	1,994,199	337,419
8	646,064	4,977	8,708	13,685	109,911	1,922,156	336,013
9	629,966	4,940	8,663	13,603	109,485	1,852,681	334,620
10	613,845	4,905	8,687	13,592	109,484	1,792,097	334,018
11	597,764	4,872	8,644	13,516	109,089	1,727,088	332,487
12	582,141	4,826	8,596	13,422	108,623	1,664,230	330,927
13	566,283	4,852	8,537	13,389	108,220	1,604,306	329,562
14	551,267	4,816	8,501	13,317	107,916	1,547,121	328,356
15	536,718	4,785	8,516	13,301	107,894	1,496,177	328,008
16	535,223	4,787	8,229	13,016	107,277	1,622,446	326,816
17	518,878	4,768	8,112	12,880	108,396	1,571,291	327,140
18	508,157	4,765	8,176	12,941	108,968	1,502,227	328,093
19	497,339	4,802	8,169	12,971	109,503	1,468,547	328,705
20	482,198	4,796	8,056	12,852	108,124	1,401,488	325,621
21	471,256	4,833	8,110	12,943	108,628	1,353,489	326,251
22	460,345	4,871	8,137	13,008	109,016	1,306,620	326,730
23	449,495	4,850	8,160	13,010	109,365	1,260,731	327,001
24	438,938	4,884	8,180	13,064	109,641	1,215,541	327,114

21st Year Increase	Cash Value 30th Year	Estate Value Age 55	Cash Value Age 55	Increase Age 55	Increase Age 65	Red. Inc. CV age65
$20,454	$616,480	$7,348,589	$2,850,067	$166,543	$243,030	$140,659
20,572	618,879	6,940,457	2,697,203	157,751	230,429	134,390
20,771	619,437	6,532,652	2,543,711	148,903	217,715	127,865
20,752	619,211	6,138,883	2,395,245	140,331	205,396	121,489
20,971	618,439	5,763,066	2,252,973	132,101	193,535	115,203
20,507	611,369	5,352,106	2,096,458	123,031	180,408	108,051
20,430	609,721	5,012,833	1,967,241	115,542	169,578	102,164
20,328	607,991	4,693,636	1,844,795	108,422	159,236	96,373
20,298	606,448	4,393,094	1,730,326	101,782	149,636	91,102
20,249	605,346	4,113,534	1,623,680	95,591	140,683	86,161
20,277	605,606	3,859,771	1,526,666	89,953	132,523	81,605
20,250	604,622	3,613,353	1,432,401	84,474	124,583	77,164
20,235	602,512	3,376,145	1,341,639	79,198	116,936	72,854
20,158	601,151	3,158,094	1,258,001	74,331	109,873	68,845
20,040	599,130	2,950,418	1,178,353	69,701	103,147	65,004
20,152	599,134	2,766,426	1,107,617	65,585	97,159	61,562
20,329	603,666	2,888,458	1,054,635	62,760	101,970	64,871
20,496	604,745	2,710,287	991,943	59,077	96,051	61,386
20,674	606,648	2,545,200	934,481	55,671	90,666	58,287
20,775	607,491	2,386,064	879,022	52,420	85,459	55,271
20,654	601,204	2,210,175	817,274	48,797	79,635	51,830
20,626	601,526	2,070,069	768,246	45,927	75,019	49,111
20,666	601,608	1,938,618	722,155	42,904	70,669	46,537
20,692	601,137	1,814,463	678,546	40,024	66,527	44,068
20,677	600,295	1,698,025	637,593	37,298	62,603	41,723

YOU DON'T HAVE TO DIE TO WIN

Age	Premium $10,000 Face Amount	1st Year Cash Value	2nd Year Increase	Total	Cash Value 10th Year	Estate Value 20th Year	Cash Value 20th Year
25	428,473	4,869	8,315	13,184	111,153	1,185,626	330,218
26	418,121	4,896	8,315	13,211	111,367	1,143,182	330,201
27	407,723	4,920	8,354	13,274	111,542	1,102,399	330,125
28	397,490	4,931	8,340	13,271	111,658	1,063,215	330,123
29	387,599	4,904	8,402	13,306	111,672	1,025,438	329,842
30	377,881	4,908	8,450	13,358	112,652	997,213	331,849
31	368,203	4,947	8,457	13,404	112,609	961,885	331,505
32	358,733	4,912	8,502	13,414	112,557	927,904	331,066
33	349,215	4,909	8,507	13,416	112,445	895,280	330,569
34	339,818	4,936	8,475	13,411	112,243	863,667	329,933
35	321,908	4,932	8,499	13,431	112,674	837,539	330,680
36	321,170	4,930	8,525	13,455	112,426	808,110	329,817
37	313,170	4,920	8,507	13,427	112,076	779,460	328,740
38	304,596	4,912	8,524	13,436	111,763	752,355	327,696
39	296,197	4,900	8,495	13,395	111,348	726,032	326,434
40	287,893	4,879	8,499	13,378	111,507	704,355	326,484
41	279,958	4,858	8,468	13,326	111,058	680,112	325,072
42	272,052	4,869	8,435	13,304	110,621	656,913	323,558
43	264,282	4,845	8,396	13,241	110,084	634,550	321,883
44	256,660	4,822	8,381	13,203	109,563	613,247	320,167
45	249,134	4,799	8,346	13,145	109,664	595,660	319,730
46	241,785	4,776	8,332	13,108	109,115	575,901	317,813
47	237,183	4,779	8,348	13,127	108,512	556,176	315,756
48	230,116	4,755	8,321	13,076	107,924	538,023	313,661
49	225,670	4,727	8,378	13,105	107,329	520,289	311,566
50	218,801	4,726	8,322	13,048	106,769	503,891	309,368
51	212,097	4,700	8.266	12,966	105,860	487,072	306,410
52	207,713	4,685	8,300	12,985	104,989	471,017	303,589
53	201,271	4,647	8,270	12,917	104,010	455,438	300,241
54	198,226	4,661	8,317	12,978	103,473	442,155	298,128
55	193,860	4,676	8,305	12,981	103,131	429,660	295,889
56	188,710	4,676	8,239	12,965	102,510	417,284	293,145
57	182,410	4,632	8,252	12,884	101,533	404,001	289,233
58	176,236	4,581	8,212	12,793	100,620	391,060	285,065
59	170,233	4,568	8,172	12,740	99,719	378,132	280,459

21st Year Increase	Cash Value 30th Year	Estate Value Age 55	Cash Value Age 55	Increase Age 55	Increase Age 65	Red. Inc CV Age65
20,854	604,974	1,606,143	604,974	35,215	59,423	39,796
20,824	603,703	1,503,682	568,787	33,075	55,912	37,669
20,794	602,280	1,407,700	534,788	31,070	52,602	35,651
20,753	600,680	1,318,122	502,983	29,194	49,496	33,739
20,681	598,668	1,233,750	472,991	27,419	46,555	31,926
20,752	600,418	1,163,661	447,863	25,936	43,932	30,269
20,718	598,083	1,089,494	421,359	24,365	41,351	28,661
20,649	595,217	1,019,476	396,291	22,876	38,902	27,121
20,555	592,040	953,884	372,715	21,591	36,501	25,591
20,434	588,317	891,833	350,356	20,434	34,017	23,974
20,528	587,837	837,539	330,680	30,581	31,841	22,545
20,376	583,646	770,511	299,404	28,626	29,668	21,119
20,110	578,847	708,434	270,040	22,503	27,853	19,943
19,851	574,042	655,980	246,821	22,202	26,160	18,842
19,643	569,259	608,647	223,796	22,135	24,584	17,811
19,505	566,412	568,445	201,879	20,549	23,195	16,891
19,272	560,822	528,867	180,597	19,073	21,798	15,967
19,038	555,005	492,622	160,849	17,733	20,589	15,171
18,717	548,379	459,043	142,429	16,602	19,464	14,427
18,464	541,978	427,678	125,197	15,634	18,464	13,762
18,291	537,637	399,835	109,664	14,767	28,588	22,419
18,019	530,706	371,466	94,429	13,803	26,758	21,127
17,736	523,978	344,465	80,304	12,839	22,167	17,796
17,418	516,868	319,350	67,103	11,905	20,596	17,038
17,102	509,999	296,073	55,067	10,950	21,546	18,360
16,614	501,919	274,467	43,982	10,059	19,815	16,952
16,232	493,366	254,065	33,692	10,592	18,279	15,697
15,870	485,562	236,177	23,105	10,120	16,919	14,597
15,467	476,801	218,306	·12,917	8,270	15,665	13,554
15,150	470,655	204,846	4,661		13,714	12,723
14,812	464,126	193,860			13,632	11,876
14,453	456,854				12,660	11,059
14,038	448,024				11,734	10,272
13,617	438,697				10,856	9,523
13,188	428,693				10,044	8,826

Age	Premium $10,000 Face Amount	1st Year Cash Value	2nd Year Increase	Total	Cash Value 10th Year	Estate Value 20th Year	Cash Value 20th Year
60	164,462	4,583	8,149	12,732	98,998	365,544	275,664
61	158,967	4,597	8,114	12,711	98,459	353,608	270,914
62	153,686	4,606	8,088	12,694	98,222	342,359	266,272
63	148,677	4,619	8,082	12,701	98,297	331,714	261,729
64	143,922	4,638	8,078	12,716	98,714	321,549	257,217
65	139,325	4,655	8,090	12,745	99,535	311,769	252,666
66	134,720	4,,727	8,176	12,903	99,364	302,170	248,023
67	129,712	4,795	88,278	13,073	97,612	292,001	242,586
68	135,713	4,913	8,445	13,358	96,028	282,690	237,518
69	121,369	5,032	8,648	13,680	94,479	274,310	232,923
70	117,790	5,138	8,597	12,735	93,174	266,699	228,672
71	113,865	5,089	8,414	13,503	91,400	258,056	223,257
72	109,406	5,171	8,272	12,443	86,699	249,237	217,443
73	104,972	5,104	8,077	13,181	87,602	239,969	211,097
74	100,485	5,028	7,898	12,926	85,565	230,883	204,887
75	95,231	4,933	7,655	12,588	83,121	220,805	197,890
76	90,033	4,847	7,421	12,268	80,831	211,260	191,694
77	84,523	4,750	7,173	11,923	78,548	201,751	185,971
78	78,779	4,654	6,922	11,576	76,362	192,450	180,988
79	73,946	4,583	6,738	11,321	75,253	186,528	180,025
80	68,828	4,521	6,554	11,075	75,571	185,233	185,233

21st Year Increase	Cash Value 30th Year	Estate Value Age 55	Cash Value Age 55	Increase Age 55	Increase Age 65	Red. Inc CV Age65
12,757	418,517					8,170
12,347	408,545					8,949
11,944	298,764					8,607
11,557	389,349					7,193
11,182	380,626					
11,944	381,780					
11,568	374,945					
11,157	368,861					
10,766	365,331					
10,448	364,842					
10,105	367,970					
9,723						
9,396						
9,203						
9,163						
9,343						
9,697						
10,197						
10,971						
12,607						

1. Assume you are twenty-five years old earning $40,000 gross income.
2. Bank's lending criteria: 35 per cent net debt ratio, 40 per cent gross debt ratio, the other 60 per cent is for living expenses and income tax.
3. My formula: 25 per cent of gross, leaving margin for emergency.
4. If you use your policies as your operating account, you can effectively earn compound interest on your operating account and be able to retire on $35,215 after tax at age fifty-five, or $59,423 after tax at age sixty-five, without upsetting your life insurance.
5. Remember, this is only a formula.
6. Cash values are subject to any indebtedness you may have incurred to sustain your lifestyle.

About the Author

Robert (Bob) Shiels was born in Edinburgh, Scotland, in 1929. He was only ten years old when his father died, leaving his mother to bring up three children, of whom Bob was the eldest. Perhaps his positive attitude towards life insurance stems from the fact that he witnessed his mother struggle for most of the rest of her life determined that her family suffered as little as possible, although she had neither husband nor a life insurance settlement to help her.

Granted a scholarship to George Herriot's, one of Edinburgh's finest public schools, Bob had the advantage of a good education but, unfortunately, as the eldest child of the family, he had to leave school at a relatively early age to help his mother support the family. While his first job was gained in no small way through his old-school tie, it was his drive and determination that saw him appointed as Works Manager at James Ross and Sons, manufacturing confectioners, by the time he was twenty-one.

At the age of twenty-four the grass seemed greener on the other side of the Atlantic so he resigned his post and sailed to Toronto in 1953. He started work at his original trade as a manufacturer confectioner at Rowntrees on Sterling Road making Smarties. Then he worked one year in customer service at Canadian General Electric, and sold real estate with Harvey on the Danforth until 1955 when he moved to St. Catharines. He spent three and a half years selling Mammy's Bread until 1959 when he joined London Life Insurance Company, and has been with the company ever since.

In 1974 he remarried, and he and his wife Anne still live in St. Catharines where they enjoy a busy social life.

Life insurance has been Bob's business for fifty years, and it is fair to say that he practises what he preaches.

One of his biggest regrets is that his mother did not live to enjoy the fruits of his success.

Glossary

Cash flow: Your net income minus your regular expenses (mortgage/rent, food etc.)

Cash value: This is the guaranteed amount available in cash from a policy each year. Of this amount, 90 to 95 per cent is available for borrowing directly from your insurance company at your own flexible repayment terms.

Cash value of paid-up additions: This figure forms part of the total cash value of any policy. It is the cash value of a life insurance option that allows the insured to use policy dividends to purchase additional limits of whole life insurance coverage that are paid in full (paid up).

Convertible Term Life Insurance: Most term life insurance policies are convertible. The convertibility option lets you exchange your term life policy for a whole life policy.

Deductible interest charges: Any interest on money borrowed for investment purposes is tax deductible. Examples or investments that qualify for deductible interest charges are term deposits, bonds, stocks, shares, and investments for business purposes.

Equity: This is the value on an item minus the amount owing against it. For example, if the value of your home is $100,000 and your mortgage is for $80,000 then the equity on your home is $20,000. Other examples of equity or semi-liquid assets would be in cars, boats, furnishings, and even in an RRSP. An RRSP is considered semi-liquid because, although you can cash it in, you have to pay income tax on the proceeds.

Liquid assets: Assets that can be readily converted into cash. Examples of liquid assets include term deposits, bonds, and cash value of life insurance policies.

Liquidity: The ability or ease with which assets can be converted into cash.

Non-deductible interest charges: Interest on loans for items such as cars, vacations, consumer goods, insurance, and non-investment items on which the income is deferred.

Paid-up additions: The additional paid-up insurance that is purchased by the dividend, which is declared each year. This is a dividend option that increases coverage and helps fight inflation. The additional insurance has a cash value that may be used for borrowing purposes at the same time as the policy, and has the same flexible repayment terms.

Reasonable request: Most bankers will consider any presentation where the repayment schedule will totally retire the loan, or the loan is fully secured by liquidity, within a three-year period.

Registered Retirement Savings Plan (RRSP): A provision in the *Income Tax Act* whereby a person may shelter financial property from income taxes and provide tax benefits for saving for retirement in Canada.

Tax-Free Savings Account: An account as of 2009 where Canadians over the age of eighteen may put up to $5,000 a year to shelter tax. Although income earned in the TFSA is tax free, you won't get a tax refund for the amount invested as you would with an RRSP. The money can also be withdrawn tax-free at any time.

Term Deposits: An interest-generating method of saving over a relatively short term. These term deposits can be purchased from banks and trust companies, and are on thirty, sixty, or ninety-day terms; or one-, three-, and five-year terms. The rate of interest is fixed for the term chosen. Providing that the amount exceeds $5,000 the principal may be moved on a thirty-day basis. If the amount is less than $5,000 the term must be one year or more.